HUNTING GIRLS

HUNTING GIRLS

Sexual Violence from *The Hunger Games* to Campus Rape

KELLY OLIVER

COLUMBIA UNIVERSITY PRESS / NEW YORK

Columbia University Press
Publishers Since 1893
New York   Chichester, West Sussex
cup.columbia.edu

Library of Congress Cataloging-in-Publication Data
Names: Oliver, Kelly, 1958- author.
Title: Hunting girls : sexual violence from "The hunger games" to campus
    rape / Kelly Oliver.
Description: New York : Columbia University Press, [2016] | Includes
    bibliographical references and index.
Identifiers: LCCN 2015046456 | ISBN 9780231178365 (cloth : alk. paper) |
    ISBN 9780231541763 (ebook)
Subjects: LCSH: Mass media and sex. | Sex crimes. | Young women—Sexual
    behavior. | Young women—Violence against. | Sex in mass media. | Sex role
    in mass media. | Mass media and women.
Classification: LCC P96.S45 O45 2016 | DDC 305.42—dc23
LC record available at http://lccn.loc.gov/2015046456

Columbia University Press books are printed on permanent and durable
acid-free paper.

Printed in the United States of America

c 10 9 8 7 6 5 4 3 2 1

Cover design: Andrew Brozyna
Cover image: National Gallery of Canada, Ottawa, Ontario, Canada/
    Bridgeman Images

FOR MONECA

CONTENTS

ACKNOWLEDGMENTS

THANKS TO JULIANA LEWIS and Sarah Gorman for research assistance. Thanks to Chloë Taylor for extremely helpful comments on an earlier draft. A version of the second chapter was published as "Rape as Spectator Sport and *Creepshot* Entertainment: Social Media and the Valorization of Lack of Consent" in *American Studies Journal,* Occasional Papers (10): (Fall 2015). A shorter version of the last chapter was published as "Hunting Girls: Patriarchal Fantasy or Feminist Progress?" in *Americana: The Journal of American Popular Culture* 12 (1): (Spring 2013). As always, thanks to Beni for everything.

HUNTING GIRLS

INTRODUCTION

GIRLS AS TROPHIES

IN THE FALL OF 2012, the popular television show *America's Next Top Model* devoted a season to college girls. The thirteen finalists moved into a "sorority house" in Hollywood. One of the competitions featured a mysterious photo shoot. Beforehand, the contestants were told that the "challenge will leave you hanging," and to "make sure you kill the shot." The photo shoot was at a taxidermist's lair where the college women were posed as big-game trophies, with their heads mounted on the wall. Shot in a room with one wall completely filled with mounted animal heads—including deer, antelope, elk, and moose—the girls stuck their heads through wooden frames.

Mimicking the animals on the wall, they stared wide-eyed into the camera with their mouths slightly open, as if surprised to be "dead." The camera repeatedly cut between the girls' mounted heads, shots from behind of their decapitated bodies clad in nearly

FIGURE I.1 *America's Next Top Model*: Mounted coed photographed at taxidermist.

sheer bodysuits, and the dead animals that surrounded them. The soundtrack featured animal sounds as some of the girls posed for the photo shoot. Later, back at the studio, the judges evaluated the photographs. In the words of one judge, they wanted "dead but intensity." One of the top-scoring models was praised with

FIGURE I.2 *America's Next Top Model*: Posed to look like a dead animal.

"your eyes have an intensity but also a blankness as if your soul is gone"; while others were criticized: "you needed to be dead smize, not alive smize" ("smize" being judge Tyra Banks's neologism for smiling eyes). Another model was praised for looking like "the witch from Snow White"—Maleficent with her hair styled into two giant horns on top of her head. When one of the girls complained that the wooden frame was hurting her, the photographer replied, "Uncomfortable beauty is what we're going for." Praised for looking dead, these girls were subjected to this awkward scene for reality television, and for the resulting trophy photographs, judged as part of a "beauty contest."

It's not news that beautiful women are treated as trophies. In this photo shoot, however, their status as hunted prey is made explicit. These college girls were treated as animal prey shot dead by the camera for mounted trophies. The camera becomes the weapon in the hunt for beautiful dead girls. In light of creepshots of unconscious girls looking "dead" on Facebook sites posted by fraternities, and several high-profile rape cases involving unconscious girls described as "dead" by their rapists, bystanders, and the media, it is both stunning, and yet not surprising, that a popular reality television show would feature college girls as mounted trophies. After all, "corpse chic" has replaced "heroin chic" as the latest fashion trend. (Photos of women, or parts of women's bodies, taken without their knowledge—and therefore obviously without their consent—are called "creepshots.") Moreover, fashion photography has a long history of depicting young women as bloodied, bruised, tortured, and corpse-like. Famous fashion photographers such as Helmut Newton, Guy Bourdin, and Steven Klein nearly specialize in images of violence toward women in sexy and sexual poses (Sauers 2012). In 2007, following this trend, *America's Top Model* featured contestants as murder victims, many of them scantily clad in lingerie, as if they had been sexually assaulted before their murders. The "dead girl" trope is still popular in fashion magazines and on Internet porn sites. For example, Victoria Beckman's Autumn 2015 *Lookbook* photo shoot features models posing as unconscious, lying on the ground, or draped over chairs. Snuff porn and various varieties of pornography feature incapacitated girls and women, some looking dead. And, of course, there are fraternity photos of unconscious nude or semi-clad girls in embarrassing poses on closed Facebook sites across the country.

Unfortunately, images of bruised, abused, or "dead" women and girls as high fashion or in advertising are nothing new. As Margi Laird McCue observes: "Striking examples of the depiction of women as sex objects who deserve to be battered are often found in advertising. In the late 1980s, for instance, many fashion ads featured women who were abused, bound and gagged, or in body bags. . . . Mainstream magazine fashion layouts featured women pulled along by corset ties, their necks in choke collars; trussed and restrained in straitjackets and straps; blindfolded; and sometimes stuffed in garbage bags. One Esprit ad depicted a woman on an ironing board with a man about to iron her crotch; a Foxy Lady ad showed a woman who had been knocked to the floor with her shirt ripped open; and a Michael Mann ad pictured a woman in a coffin" (2008). Other examples include a Bill Blass ad from 1966 that features a model posing as a dead woman tied to the front grill of a car. In 2007, a highly stylized Dolce & Gabbana ad depicts a group of young men around a shirtless man who is pinning a woman to the ground, suggesting gang rape. A 2006 Jimmy Choo ad shows a dead woman in the trunk of a car. A 2008 ad for a designer men's clothing line by Duncan Quinn features a man in a suit smirking into the camera while dragging an unconscious woman (wearing only her underwear) across the hood of a car, a necktie tied around her neck. And in 2012 *Pop* magazine featured a photograph of sixteen-year-old model, Hailey Clauson, being choked by an unseen man (Sauer 2012). The list goes on and on. And this put forth as so-called *high* culture. Pornography, of course, is notoriously filled with images of abuse of women, most especially sexual assault and rape (Timberg 2013).

CREEPSHOTS OF UNCONSCIOUS GIRLS

Life imitates art, and vice versa. Thus, art often revolves around the objectification and assault of girls and women. Unfortunately, increasingly, life imitates pornography, particularly creepshot photographs of unsuspecting girls and women. With uncanny regularity, college and university officials are discovering Facebook pages, and other social media, used by fraternities, or creepshooters off the street, to post photographs of women, sometimes unconscious, naked, or in compromising positions. For example, at Penn State, one fraternity was suspended from its national chapter after a police investigation turned up pictures of drugs, hazing, and nude, unconscious women (Garrity & Blinder 2015). According to the *New York Times*, "Pledges were required to make stories with pornographic images and a 'sex position of the day.' Members regularly posted embarrassing photographs of women in 'extremely compromising' positions and used demeaning language to describe them" (Southall 2015:A13). One detective said that, in some photos, women were "passed out and nude or in other sexual or embarrassing positions. It appears from the photos provided that the individuals in the photos are not aware that the photos had been taken" (Garrity & Blinder 2015). This is not an isolated case.

Photographs of nude or semi-naked women, unconscious, taken without their knowledge, end up on social media sites, especially sites devoted to pornography and creepshots, and are remarkably popular on the Internet. Even the word *creepshot* suggests that women are being shot, not with guns, but with cameras. Unsuspecting girls and women are prey for creep-hunters looking for the best shot to post online. Even more disturbing are recordings and creepshot photographs of "party rapes" taken by perpetrators and bystanders. There are several notorious cases of videos or snapshots of unconscious girls being dragged, undressed, prodded, peed on, written on, and/or penetrated with fingers and objects, or raped—a high school girl in Steubenville (Ohio), referred to by her rapists as a "dead girl"; a college girl on a beach in Panama City (Florida), who was drugged and then raped while bystanders watched and recorded; teenaged Rehteah Parsons, who committed suicide after photographs of her being raped circulated online; Audrie Potts, another suicide after photographs of her semi-naked body went viral at her high school; and then there was the Vanderbilt University rape case where police finally convinced a college junior that she'd been gang-raped by her boyfriend and his football player buddies by showing her videos and photographs the perpetrators took of her, which they had sent around to friends.

A documentary about rape on campus entitled *The Hunting Ground* (2015) presents colleges and universities as hunting grounds for serial rapists who prey on unsuspecting women, especially freshman. Campuses are dangerous places for girls and young women. First, perhaps surprisingly, rape myths are higher on campuses than in the general population. Rape myths include the notions that girls and women are "asking for it" if they wear provocative clothing and/or that they enjoy being raped. Second, college administrations are not equipped to deal with rape and often don't respond quickly or effectively. *The Hunting Ground* records the testimony of dozens of college women who recount difficulties dealing with college administrators when they report sexual assault. In many cases, their claims are dismissed or ignored. Third, studies show that most rapists are serial rapists or repeat offenders (Lisak & Miller 2002). On college campuses, sexual predators learn that they can force sex on girls and women and get away with it. In one study, half the college men surveyed said they had used force on a date; and in another study, over 30 percent of men surveyed said they would force a woman to have sex and yet didn't consider this rape. Obviously, for these college boys and men, the boundary between sex and rape has been blurred. Fourth, drugs and/or alcohol are involved in most rapes on campus. When drugs and/or alcohol are involved, reporting rates are so low as to be almost nonexistent (Lisak & Miller 2002; Wolitzky-Taylor et al. 2011). If most rapes are committed when the victim is under the influence of drugs or alcohol, and the reporting rate in these cases is near zero, then the actual numbers of girls sexually assaulted on college campuses must be mind-boggling. Fifth, there are very few consequences for the perpetrators of sexual assault, especially if they are well-respected fraternity brothers or college athletes. Very few college boys and men found guilty of sexual assault face any punishment whatsoever. Criminal prosecution is nearly nonexistent. Further, hearings at colleges and universities rarely result in expulsion. Finally, girls and women who do report sexual assault are often harassed and face retaliation on campus. Some eventually drop out of school, a few even commit suicide. Many girls and women report that the harassment they face after the assault is worse than the assault itself. The fact that these women's victimization and pain is not taken seriously compounds the trauma of sexual assault. All of these factors make colleges and universities dangerous places for college women when it comes to sexual assault.

In the words of a junior at George Washington University (not featured in the documentary *The Hunting Ground*), "At frat parties, it's more of a hunting ground. Not all guys are like this, of course, but sometimes it feels like the lions standing in the background and looking at the deer. And then they go in for the kill" (Schwarz 2015). Girls are treated as prey by sexual predators, who often use drugs and alcohol to trap them.[1] But these sexual predators are not scary men jumping out of the bushes at night. They are clean-cut fraternity brothers, honors students, and star athletes. These are the promising young men sitting next to their prey in English class or calculus. They are the clean-cut guys at the end of the table in the student union. They may be the head of their class, or president of their fraternities, or leading athletes. These are not the mythical depraved black men supposedly raping white women so popular in the imaginations of conservatives and reactionaries. For the most part, these are young middle-class white men—the boys next door—raping middle-class white women, the girls next door. Perhaps this is why, until recently, sexual violence on campus has received little serious media attention. There is reluctance to believe that these all-American boys are capable of rape. There is the notion that "boys will be boys" when it comes to sexual assault. Within a culture that still has not shaken off its patriarchal heritage, these men are the heirs to the future. College administrators, the general public, and the media have resisted the idea that these successful college boys and men who have bright futures ahead of them might be sexual predators. Often taking the perpetrator's side over their victim's, popular sentiment too often has been that the men are the ones harmed by rape charges, that they have the most to lose, which assumes, of course, that their futures matter more than those of their victim's.

The prevalence of cellphone cameras, however, is changing the way we view sexual assault, especially when the cellphone camera becomes part of the assault. Social media may be changing attitudes toward rape. On the one hand, there is a valorization of rape and lack of consent, evidenced by creepshot photographs and the fact that perpetrators take pictures of their rapes as part of the "fun." The photographs are supposedly taken with the victim's consent and that is part of what makes them "funny," and why perpetrators share them with friends. On the other hand, cellphone photographs give investigators hard evidence that is taken seriously, even when a girl or woman's testimony might not be. In the words of one detective assigned to the Vanderbilt rape case, "pictures don't lie." The implication, of course, is that girls do. Throughout *Hunting Girls*, we will consider the contradictory ways in which social media is changing our attitudes toward sexual assault and the reporting of rape.

While using drugs and alcohol to incapacitate girls and women in order to sexually assault them is not new, taking creepshots of their naked bodies and posting them online on social media sites is new.[2] The effects of social media on rape culture go beyond exacerbating the harms of rape. Social media not only extend the harm and trauma of the assault into the future in ways that make it more difficult for victims to heal, but also photographs of sexual assaults and party rape have become a new form of pornography. In fact, in some of the high-profile cases mentioned above, perpetrators have been charged with disseminating child pornography. Even in the Vanderbilt case where the victim was twenty-one years old, the photographs themselves were part of the crime since they were taken and disseminated without her consent. Photographs taken as part of the sexual assault and posted online as trophies or further abuse have become evidence in criminal trials. Spectacles of party rape circulated for "entertainment" haunt and shame victims to the point that some take their own lives. In many of the aforementioned cases, since the girls were unconscious at the time of their rapes, they found out about them through social media, or by being shown photographs of themselves in compromising positions.

The girls and young women in Steubenville or Panama Beach, at Vanderbilt, or those featured on the Facebook page of the Penn State fraternity, all found out about their sexual assaults through third parties who showed them images of themselves passed out and abused. The impact on victims of discovering that they have been raped while unconscious is profound.[3] Given that women's testimony to their own victimization is often discounted, it is telling that the impact on the public of these photographs of girls unable to give clear and coherent testimony is also profound. Creepshot photographs of sexual assault enter a complex web of pornography, entertainment, social media, harassment and shaming of victims, and criminal evidence that can be used in court to convict perpetrators. The irony is that in some of these cases, the victims are unconscious and unaware of the sexual assault such that what is often viewed in court or in hearings as a "he said, she said" account of what happened becomes a case of the perpetrator accidently providing hard evidence in cases where "she" was unconscious and cannot testify to what happened. The perpetrator, or in these cases, usually perpetrators in the plural, provide a reliable witness in the eye of the camera. Two of the central themes of *Hunting Girls* are the role of the camera in sexual assault and the rape of unconscious victims. Not only do creepshot photos and unconscious party rape go together as new forms of entertainment, but also they are on the rise, to the point that some call party rape an "epidemic" on college campuses (Carey et al. 2015; Filipovic 2015).

PARTY RAPE

Given the use of alcohol and rape drugs that render girls and young women unconscious, the incidence of unconscious rape is truly incalculable on college campuses. First, women may not even know they were assaulted. They may wake up wondering but never sure. Second, conscious or not, the rate of reporting when alcohol is involved is only 2.7 percent (Lisak & Miller 2002; Wolitzky-Taylor et al. 2011). In the last decade or so (since about 2005), the prevalence of alcohol-accompanied sexual assault has led the U.S. Department of Justice to identify a distinct type of rape, "party rape," which is defined as one that "occurs at an off-campus house or on or off campus fraternity and involves . . . plying a woman with alcohol or targeting an intoxicated woman" (Sampson 2002:6; Armstrong et al. 2006:484). Party rape is classified as a form of acquaintance rape, even if the perpetrator and the victim are strangers. In terms of sexual assault, party rape makes colleges and universities "hunting grounds" for sexual predators, many of whom never consider their activities rape, and most of whom never consider themselves rapists.

Party rape, however, is not just the result of alcohol consumption. A combination of factors comes to bear in rape on college campuses. Certainly, not every man who parties is a rapist and not every woman who parties is a rape victim. One study concludes: "Cultural expectations that partygoers drink heavily and trust party-mates become problematic when combined with expectations that women be nice and defer to men. Fulfilling the role of the partier produces vulnerability on the part of women, which some men exploit to extract nonconsensual sex" (Armstrong et al. 2006).[4] This study also finds that multiple variables, including individual psychology, rape myths and rape culture, and particular contexts such as fraternities rife with gender inequalities lead to rape (Armstrong et al. 2006:484–85). The use of rape drugs to intentionally incapacitate college women is particularly reprehensible insofar as it is not only premeditated rape, but also because these drugs are in themselves dangerous, even lethal in high doses (Zorza 2001). In 2014, at the University of Wisconsin, for example, several girls ended up in the hospital after they were served punch spiked with Rohypnol at a fraternity party (Mejia 2014). This fraternity engaged in a "rape conspiracy" by planning sexual assault and intentionally drugging unsuspecting women. As long as college men continue to see women as sexual prey or trophies, rape will continue to plague college campuses.

As we have seen, addressing party rape is compounded by the problem that women don't report it. Women are much less likely to report sexual assault if it occurs when they are intoxicated because they are unclear about what happened and/or do not feel entitled to report it since they were drunk (Adams-Curtis & Forbes 2004; Armstrong et al. 2006). As I mentioned earlier, some may not even know they were assaulted, or they may be unsure. In addition, given the increasingly slippery slope between sex and sexual assault, and uncertainty about what counts as rape, many women are subject to sexual aggression, even sexual assault, and are not sure whether or not they have been raped (Burnett et al. 2009). Because the progression from "sexual negotiation to coercion is commonplace in the college setting" (Burnett et al. 2009), survivors question their own consent and their own responsibility for unwanted sexual contact (Adams-Curtis & Forbes 2004). One study reports that half of the men surveyed admitted to using some form of sexual aggression on a date (Wolitzky-Taylor et al. 2011:582). Finally, even when women are certain that they have been assaulted, when drugs or alcohol are involved they are more likely to buy into the rape myths that blame the victims. Or, if the drugs are illegal, or the girls are underage for drinking, they may not want to admit that they were engaging in these criminal activities, so they don't report being assaulted.

It is not just access to drugs and alcohol that foster rape culture on college campuses, but also the acceptance of rape myths is higher on college campuses than it is in the general population. As one study concludes, "college campuses foster date rape cultures, which are environments that support beliefs conducive to rape and increase risk factors related to sexual violence" (Burnett et al. 2009).[5] The existence of rape myths such as "victims are responsible for their own rapes," or "victims are sluts and are asking for it," or that "no" really means "yes" are prevalent on college campuses and part of the culture of fraternities and sports cultures. Although colleges and universities are institutions of higher learning, producing the most educated people in the country, they also breed rape myths at a higher rate than other cultural institutions. These attitudes, along with a lack of attention on the part of administrators, and a lack of consequences for perpetrators, is why campuses are so dangerous for young women. One study concludes, "Athletics and fraternal organizations, replete on college campuses, are related to stronger rape-supportive attitudes, based on such myths" (Burnett et al. 2009).[6] This study, among others, shows how college athletics and fraternity culture perpetuate a classic double standard whereby men who have sex, even force sex, are "studs," whereas women who have sex are sluts (Burnett et al. 2009; see also Adams-Curtis & Forbes 2004). In addition, several studies indicate that aggressive sports are correlated with aggressive sex: "College men who play aggressive sports in high school are more likely to accept rape myths, are more accepting of violence, and engage in more sexual coercion toward dating partners compared to other college men" (Forbes et al. 2006; Burnett et al. 2009). The combination of a party atmosphere with alcohol flowing, and the acceptance of rape myths that include blaming the victim or the fantasy that victims enjoy rape—myths that are perpetuated by fraternities and in jock culture—makes colleges and universities especially fertile hunting grounds for serial rapists and men who are willing to force sex.

Newsweek magazine reports that "nearly one-third of college men admit they might rape a woman if they could get away with it" (Bekiempis 2015). As it turns out, this is a telling misrepresentation of the results of the study, which found that approximately 32 percent of college men said they would force a woman to have sex, but only 13 percent of those said they would rape a woman (Edwards et al. 2014). This demonstrates the power of the word *rape*. It also shows that the majority of men who would force a woman to have sex don't consider it rape. Indeed, if recent revelations brought to light via social media photos and videos are any indication, groups of young people happily watch, and even record, unconscious women being sexually assaulted without intervening or calling police. As mentioned earlier, in another study, half of college men admit to using aggressive tactics to have sex (Wolitzky-Taylor et al. 2011:582). If you are a woman of a certain age reading this book, it is likely that you have experienced pressure by men to have sex, or that you have been coerced into doing something that you didn't really want to do, or that you have been sexually assaulted.

Of course, rape happens on and off college campuses. So why focus on rape on campus, and party rape in particular? Studies show that the chances of being raped are higher on college campuses than off, at least for young women. "Every two minutes in the United States, someone is raped, and the chances of being that victim are four times greater for a college female student than for any other age group" (Burnett et al. 2009). Additionally, college women are at greater risk of rape and sexual assault than the comparable age group not in college (Fisher et al. 2000; Armstrong et al. 2006). It is important to note that college men are also victims of rape. Still, the vast majority of rape victims on campus are women (Armstrong et al. 2006; Krebs et al 2009).[7] The National Center for Injury Prevention and Control estimates that one in five women are raped in college (Edwards et al. 2014). However, given that rates of reporting are so low (64 percent to 96 percent go unreported; and only 2.7 percent of rapes involving drugs or alcohol are reported), as we've seen, it is difficult to know the real numbers of sexual assault on campus, which must be much, much higher (Lisak & Miller 2002; Wolitzky-Taylor et al. 2011). In addition, with traditionally low rates of reporting, combined with changing attitudes toward reporting sexual violence, it is even more difficult to determine whether or not rape on college campuses is on the rise, or only if the reporting of rape is increasing.

Whichever is the case, rape on college campuses, especially party rape, is more visible in the media than ever before, in part thanks to social media, which not only allows victims to find each other and unite against rape on campus but also has been used to continue to victimize girls. High school and college boys are using cellphones to take photos and videos of their assaults and posting them online. Instead of helping unconscious girls who are being sexually assaulted, bystanders whip out their phones and start recording. Rape may not be new, but gleefully watching, recording, and distributing photographs of rape via social media is. As we will see, these photographs are evidence that lack of consent has become valorized and eroticized such that so-called "nonconsensual sex" is the goal for many men on college campuses. Nonconsensual sex has become a form of entertainment in our culture. Certainly lack of consent is essential to "creepshots," where websites specify that photographs must be "candid" and therefore taken unbeknownst to the subject.

As numerous high-profile cases of party rape among college and high school students make clear, if attitudes toward rape are making it easier for women to come forward and report their victimization—which is debatable—they also are making rape a kind of "fun" spectator sport, full of "Kodak moments," now "Facebook moments," to be photographed, recorded, and posted onto social media for added entertainment. Images of unconscious girls being abused and sexually assaulted have been circulating on social media sites, posted by perpetrators and bystanders who obviously think they are "funny." Resonant with the photographs of would-be models posed as dead animals, these rape photographs function as displays of conquest and trophies of dominance, which show girls as "dead," like pieces of meat, to be manipulated and then photographed for entertainment.

VIOLENCE TOWARD GIRLS FROM
THE HUNGER GAMES TO *FIFTY SHADES*

Just months before the *America's Next Top Model* photo shoot featuring college coeds as mounted trophies, the film version of the popular Young Adult novel, *The Hunger Games* (2012), broke all previous records at the box office. The film is about a sixteen-year-old girl, Katniss Everdeen, who is both hunted and hunter, predator and prey. Our pubescent protagonist, a tough no-nonsense teenager, is more comfortable wearing hunting clothes and boots than a prom dress and heels. Whatever she wears, she becomes the unwilling and unwitting star of the reality television show the "Hunger Games," a fight to the death between teens, and her every move is caught on camera and broadcast on screens for all to see. When Katniss places flowers on the dead body of her young friend Rue, the video goes viral and sparks a revolution. Katniss and her boyfriend Peeta's first kiss is replayed over and over again in a world obsessed with watching candid shots of unsuspecting teens on screens. Katniss's adolescence is a spectacle displayed for the entertainment of the corrupt Capitol city. Katniss is a symbol for coming-of-age in a violent world recorded as entertainment, a world where the assault of girls and young women is taken for granted. Although Katniss isn't sexually assaulted per se—unlike her filmic sister Beatrice "Tris" Prior (Shailene Woodley) in the Young Adult blockbuster *Divergent* (2014)—she is repeatedly abused, even by her boyfriend, who at one point tries to choke her.

Adolescent virgin girls, like Katniss, who are at home in the forest hunting animals with bows and arrows, have become new

FIGURE I.3 Katniss Everdeen (Jennifer Lawrence) hunting in *The Hunger Games* (2012), directed by Gary Ross.

cultural icons for young girls.[8] With new Artemis characters leading the way wielding bows and arrows—such as Hanna (Soarise Ronan) in *Hanna* (2011), Katniss (Jennifer Lawrence) in *The Hunger Games* (2012), Merida (voiced by Kelly Macdonald) in *Brave*

FIGURE I.4 Neytiri (Zoe Saldana) with bow in *Avatar* (2009), directed by James Cameron.

FIGURE I.5 Keira Knightley as Guinevere in *King Arthur* (2004), directed by Antoine Fuqua.

(2012), and Tauriel (Evageline Lilly) in *The Hobbit: The Desolation of Smaug* (2013)—archery among girls and women is on the rise. Women and girl hunters account for the growth of hunting sports (*The Economist* 2006; FoxNews.com 2013).[9]

FIGURE I.6 Evangeline Lilly as Tauriel in Peter Jackson's *The Hobbit: The Desolation of Smaug* (2013).

Membership in USA Archery has more than doubled, primarily with girls joining, some with pink bows, others with bows just like Katniss's recurve bow (Bachman 2011; Hood 2013). There are "Hunger Games" camps where kids pretend to kill each other in Hunger Games–style competitions (Lanfreschi 2012; Gartner, 2013). And Archery Tag is a new sport that is taking off worldwide thanks to *The Hunger Games* franchise (Anderson 2014). Archery among girls is on fire thanks to Katniss (McGowan 2013).

So, we live in a rape culture that valorizes lack of consent and sexual assault, especially of young high school and college age girls, but we also have images of ever-younger strong girls wielding weapons who can take care of themselves. What gives? Do images of self-sufficient girls signal feminist progress in terms of gender stereotypes? Are these girls heroines who won't tolerate sexual assault and can defend themselves against attack? Are tough girls in film compensatory revenge fantasies to counterbalance the violent reality of assault, especially sexual assault, in the lives of girls and women? Or does watching girls hunt and fight become the justification for abusing them, a new sort of blame-the-victim strategy wherein they have it coming because they are the truly violent ones? Most likely, these images of hunting and hunted girls do all of the above, and more. One thing is certain, images of teenage girls being repeatedly beaten and battered on screen normalizes violence toward girls and women, including sexual violence. While these films feature tough girls who can fight off their attackers and protect themselves, they also contribute to our acceptance of assault.

It is fascinating that hunting, particularly with bow and arrows, has become associated with strength in girls and women. Killing animals for food and sport, as Katniss does, proves that these girls are strong and independent. Their independence is bought through the lives of their prey. Their own status as prey is camouflaged by their position as predators in relation to the animals upon which they prey. We could say there is a displacement from girls to animals that deflects the girls' status as prey onto animals. Of course, as the *America's Next Top Model* episode featuring college girls as mounted trophies makes clear, the connection between girls and animals is vexed, and both girls and animals are considered prey worthy of trophy hunting.

Conventionally, hunting has been associated with men and masculinity, while loving animals has been associated with women, or more especially with girls, and femininity (Gaarder 2011:58–59). In film in particular, traditional princesses are always portrayed with animal companions—chipmunks, squirrels, birds, raccoons, insects, rodents, dogs, cats, frogs, lizards, and horses. How can we explain the dramatic shift in popular film from girls loving animals to girls killing animals? Certainly, one way to establish that these girls are tough, fearless, and can provide as well as a man is by showing them hunting. Traditionally in American culture, eating meat has been seen as essential for strength and substance. Even more than eating them, it is macho to hunt and kill animals, especially big game.[10] The bigger the animal, the manlier the hunt. Hunting is associated with masculinity because it is a way of providing for the family, and because it is a blood sport that confirms man's position at the top of the food chain.

In *Hanna*, *The Hunger Games*, and *Twilight*, killing animals is a rite of passage for these girls on the brink of womanhood. Their relationships to animals are complex insofar as they hunt them, and yet they are seen as more akin to them than their male counterparts. In some ways, the fact that these girls stalk the forest makes them more like animals, rather than proving their position in the hierarchy at the top of the food chain. At the same time that hunting prowess makes these girls more masculine, it also reinforces their connection to nature and to animals. In these films there is nostalgia for this connection to nature and the loss of innocence signaled by technological advances that separate us from nature. Girls in these films represent our lost connection to nature. Furthermore, their loss of innocence represents the loss of innocence associated with high-tech culture. In *Hanna*, *The Hunger Games*, and *Divergent*, the innocence of our heroines is contrasted with the high-tech world of surveillance cameras and other symbols of social media such as screens that display the girls' actions and even their thoughts in the case of Tris in *Divergent*. In films such as *Hanna*, *Twilight*, and *The Hunger Games*, our heroines' hunting prowess is also a precursor to their sexual awakening. The tension between their virginity and their budding pubescent sexuality is part of their fascination and appeal. In these films, the girls' hunting skills not only enable them to survive in a hostile and often high-tech world but also make them both attractive and dangerous.

As in traditional myths and fairytales, for our new heroines, coming-of-age is full of dangers. The danger of assault, rape, and unwanted pregnancy threaten girls coming-of-age. While these dangers aren't new, the particular dangers of fighting back, and of broadcast technologies, are. Traditionally, girls are hunted but not hunters. They are prey but not predators (unless we consider stereotypes of girls and women as sexual predators, black widows, or femme fatales). In these coming-of-age stories, girls continue to face the dangers of assault, particularly sexual assault, but now they have the power to fight back, which also means they will be subject to vengeance and retaliation by their attackers. These filmic hunting girls may track down their attackers, but like girls and women on campus who fight back against sexual assault, they often face retaliation. In contemporary "fairytales," our modern heroines hunt, but they are also hunted. They are both predators and prey.

Traditionally, fairytales have been coming-of-age stories that serve as warnings of the dangers of the transition from childhood to adulthood. In the words of cultural historian and fairytale curator Erika Eichenseer, "Their main purpose was to help young adults on their path to adulthood, showing them that dangers and challenges can be overcome through virtue, prudence and courage" (qtd. in Sussens-Messerer 2012). Contemporary images of tough teenage girls coming-of-age in Hollywood blockbusters can be read as retellings of classic fairytales such as The Little Mermaid, Cinderella, Beauty and the Beast, and Sleeping Beauty. Even while these contemporary stories are new in that they give us active teen girl protagonists who defy gender stereotypes, they continue to circumscribe girls into traditional heteronormative relationships wherein they care for, and sometimes suffer at the hands of, their traumatized boyfriends. Our contemporary princesses are not waiting for their prince to save them. On the contrary, more often they save their princes, not only from physical harm but also from emotional abuses that have made these boys dangerous. In a sense, our young heroines must save their boyfriends from their own violent impulses, brainwashed into them by a violent culture. These violent lads are redeemed through the love of our goodhearted heroines.

Images of hunting girls give us less traditionally feminine protagonists, yet these films not only continue to inscribe them within traditional heterosexual romance fantasies but also subject them to increasing levels of abusive violence. This violence toward strong girls can be interpreted as punishment for their independence from men. Our new Cinderella, Katniss Everdeen, may be more like Artemis, a hunter happy in the forest, than a damsel in distress, but she is repeatedly beaten and nearly killed. Even as Hollywood gives us new images of strong empowered girls, it continues to beat them. These tough girls are bruised, bloodied, and nearly killed. On the one hand, images of hunting girls in Hollywood films show us increasingly violent female protagonists combined with increasing violence toward them. Thus, these films normalize violence against girls, including sexual violence. On the other hand, these stories take us back to classic fairytales and play on age-old myths about femininity and the transition from girlhood to womanhood.

In the filmic presentations of heroines such as Hanna (in *Hanna*), Katniss Everdeen (in *The Hunger Games*), Bella Swan (in *Twilight*), and Tris Prior (in *Divergent*), these girls who "give as good as they get" are repeatedly beaten and attacked, including by their own boyfriends. Their resistance to patriarchal stereotypes becomes justification for their abuse. Their strength in fighting back against their assailants becomes filmic justification for visually reveling in the violence done to them. The camera feasts on their abuse and aestheticizes violence toward pubescent girls. Furthermore, the violence they suffer seems to be punishment for their sexual awakening. For these girls, violence, including sexual violence, is part of their everyday existence.

While recent representations of violence toward girls and young women may speak to the lives of teenage girls today, they also function to normalize violence against girls. This normalization of violence, particularly sexual violence, is especially problematic in light of recent attention to rape in high schools and on college campuses, where by the time they graduate college, 20 percent of girls will report being sexually assaulted.[11] As classic fairytales remind us, coming-of-age has always been dangerous for girls. Even as they defy gender norms, our contemporary teenage heroines take us back to myths of classic fairytale princesses, emphasizing the violence of these tales. By aestheticizing violence against girls and young women, including and especially sexual violence, these films continue a long line of images that anesthetize us to violence against girls. From classic fairytales, to pornography, to Hollywood blockbusters aimed at teens, popular culture valorizes images of violence toward girls and women. What's new is that now our heroines are fighting back. In addition to fighting back against violence toward them, these girls must also learn to navigate the world of social media and the ways in which it exacerbates harm even while it opens up the opportunity for change. While sexual assault and rape are not new, the use of cellphone cameras and social media that turn rape into an accepted, or at least normalized, form of entertainment is new. In *The Hunger Games* and *Divergent* in particular, discerning the real from the spectacle and navigating the dangers of social media become essential for the survival of our strong girl protagonists.

In *Hunting Girls*, I analyze these films in the context of traditional fairytales and Disney princesses, on the one hand, and contemporary party rape and social media on the other. In the first and second chapters, "A Princess Is Being Beaten and Raped," and "Rape as Spectator Sport and Creepshot Entertainment," I

trace the drugging and raping of unconscious girls from the fourteenth-century legend of Sleeping Beauty, through recent Hollywood blockbusters, to contemporary party rape on campus. In
addition, I follow the problematic notion of consent from the hallucination or fantasy that an unconscious girl can consent in the
myth of Sleeping Beauty to the valorization of lack of consent in
Fifty Shades of Grey. The increasing popularity of creepshots on
the Internet is evidence of this valorization and eroticization of
a lack of consent. Some propose affirmative consent policies as
the answer. But analysis of affirmative consent apps for cellphones
make apparent many of the problems with the notion of consent
as a contractual moment that can be isolated not only from the
activities of sex but also from the social and historical context of
power dynamics in sexual relations between men and women. In
the second chapter, I discuss the complexities of consent in the
context of gendered power relations, on the one hand, and, on the
other, the party culture on college campuses that often blur lines
of consent. Highlighting the double life of creepshot photographs
and recordings of sexual assaults as forms both of bullying and
abuse, on the one hand, and as hard evidence of assaults on the
other, I discuss the telling notion that "pictures don't lie" in the
context of a culture that discounts the testimony of victims of sexual assault. In the conclusion, I suggest an alternative way of con-
ceiving of consent that takes us back to a more archaic meaning of
the Latin *con* (together, with) *sentire* (feeling) as feeling together
or a journey together that demands attention to the response from
one's partner.

In the last chapter, "Girls as Predators and Prey," I analyze Hollywood blockbuster films that feature strong empowered girls from
Twilight and *The Hunger Games* to *The Girl with the Dragon Tattoo* and *Fifty Shades of Grey* in light of both their fairytale predecessors and the real-world violence that surrounds girls making
the transition to womanhood in the age of social media. They may
have become hunters rather than princesses, but these girls continue to be hunted as trophies in a rape culture that values macho

men who take what they want through violence and domination. When girls and women fight back, this becomes justification for the increasing levels of violence done to them, as shown in recent films in ever-gorier detail to younger and younger audiences—manifest in the real world as retaliation and harassment against women who report sexual assault, and anti-rape activists on campus. Even as tough hunting girls prove themselves to be equal-opportunity killers, they continue to be beaten, battered, and assaulted. In a world where social media plays a central and complicated part in coming-of-age, our savvy heroines must learn to cope with both physical and virtual violence. They may be active instead of passive, but they are still coerced and their consent is still sometimes imagined as part of a pornographic rape fantasy. In a world where coming-of-age for girls too often includes violence, particularly sexual violence, these contemporary fairytales function as compensatory fantasies of girl power and sexual agency, even while they warn of the dangers of the transition from girlhood to womanhood.

While the cultural phenomenon that is *Fifty Shades of Grey* frontally addresses the question of consent in an age of increasing concern over nonconsensual sex on college campuses, it does so by valorizing the lack of women's consent. Lack of consent is seen as hot. While women's sexual autonomy and sexual agency are explicit messages of *Fifty Shades* and some of its Hollywood sisters, those messages continue to send mixed signals about forcing girls into sex. For example, the character "Fat Amy" (Rebel Wilson) in the trailer for *Pitch Perfect 2* (2015) sends contradictory messages when she refuses an offer of sex with a wink, signaling that "no" might really mean "yes." Even our latest tough teen heroine, Tris Prior in *Divergent*, has to fight off an attempted rape at the hands of her boyfriend, Four (Theo James). And what of Princess Tilde of Sweden, waiting bare-bottomed, asking for anal sex from the gentleman spy who rescues her in *Kingsman: The Secret Service* (2015)?

Our contemporary princess may not be Sleeping Beauty waiting for a kiss from her prince to awaken her into the world of womanhood. But our new fairytales are not as far removed from their classical sisters as we might imagine. Some of our princes are still violent, controlling, would-be rapists. Strength is still measured in terms of hunting and killing. And girls and women are still assaulted, battered, and raped. Instead of passive princesses, we have tough hunting girls like Katniss and Bella killing animals and fighting alongside their boyfriends. We have Bella Swan, and her *Fifty Shades* soft-porn alter ego Anastasia Steel, begging for sex, but they still end up bruised and physically (if not also emotionally) hurt. We have Tris Prior successfully fighting off unwanted sexual advances from her boyfriend Four, and then initiating sex later in *Divergent*. Further, we have Princess Tilde asking for it up the ass in *Kingsman*. Not your grandma's princesses: rather than passively waiting, these strong girls fight and kill like men, and sometimes they ask for kinky sex. Perhaps this signals some kind of progress. But when sexual assault has been downgraded from rape to "nonconsensual sex" on many college campuses (and in some state criminal codes), and fraternity brothers are marching around Yale openly chanting, "No means yes, yes means anal," it is crucial to ask whether this type of progress actually benefits girls and women.

1

A PRINCESS IS BEING
BEATEN AND RAPED

STRONG GIRL PROTAGONISTS IN Young Adult literature and films such as Bella Swan in *Twilight*, Katniss Everdeen in *The Hunger Games*, and Beatrice "Tris" Prior in *Divergent* give as good as they get. Still, in these contemporary fairytales, our princesses are being beaten, bloodied, bruised, almost killed, and sometimes even sexually assaulted. The rape of princesses, however, is as old as princesses themselves. And sexual assault in film is nothing new.[1] Hollywood has always banked on representations of violence toward women. Now, the women are just girls; and the abuse of teenage girls, beaten and bloodied in films, is aimed at younger and younger audiences. With film, fantasies of violence toward girls and women take on a visual dimension that further eroticize and anesthetize images of abuse toward girls. Insofar as these images of girls being beaten are staged and shot in the same way as other violent images in blockbuster films, they become part of the entertainment.[2]

Certainly, within these retold fairytales, for girls (and boys) coming-of-age is brutally violent. The transition from girlhood to womanhood is a violent initiation, which in some ways may mirror the real-world experience of girls, who, statistically, face a strong chance of becoming the victims of sexual abuse, violence, and rape.[3] Although my analysis is not directed at *hookup* culture, or even *rape* culture, per se, it interacts with those notions.[4] Specifically, I consider issues of power, control, and danger, as they play into contemporary manifestations of sexuality. In this chapter, I argue that these filmic fantasies perpetuate, justify, aestheticize, and normalize violence toward girls. In addition, some of these contemporary fantasies take us back to medieval notions of consent as the purview of men only, and thereby serve as warnings to girls and young women coming-of-age in a world of affirmative consent apps for cellphones, and party rape creepshots photographed, or recorded, on those same cellphones. Here, tracing the fantasy of consent on the part of sexual predators, along with the drugging and raping of unconscious girls, from the fourteenth-century tale of Sleeping Beauty to its contemporary retellings in Disney's *Maleficent* (2014) and *Divergent*, to the wildly popular *Fifty Shades of Grey* wherein lack of consent is hot, it becomes clear that in terms of sexual politics, in many ways, we are still in the Middle Ages.

THE RAPE OF SLEEPING BEAUTY

Once upon a time, there was a tale of a beautiful princess who was drugged unconscious and raped. What could be an entry in too many a college girl's diary is the medieval tale of Sleeping Beauty, familiar to pop culture through Disney without the drugs or rape—that is, until 2014's dark retelling in *Maleficent* (played by Angelina Jolie). The myth of Sleeping Beauty, awakened from sleep by the kiss of her prince, is the quintessential rape fantasy. Revisiting this fairytale and its history is apt considering the widespread use of rape drugs on college campuses, drugs that render girls unconscious or put them to sleep.[5] What are we to make of this desire to kiss or have sex with—that is to say, rape—an unconscious "dead" girl? For starters, it is a desire that takes us back to the fourteenth century at least, and may be the ultimate power trip for sexual predators.

The fantasy of sex with an unconscious girl is centuries old, mythical even, with its first recorded roots in an anonymous fourteenth-century Catalan story entitled *Frayre de Joy e Sor de Plaser* (Léglu 2010:102). In this version of the fairytale, after the beautiful virgin daughter of the emperor of Gint-Senay dies suddenly, her parents place her in a tower accessible by a bridge of glass. Among the young men attracted to the tower, Prince Frayre de Joy, son of King Florianda, convinces a magician to give him the means to reach the tower. When he sees the sleeping beauty's smiling face, he "has sex repeatedly with the corpse" and gets her pregnant. Nine months later, she gives birth to a son who suckles at her dead breast. The prince wants to marry Sor de Plaser and makes a bargain with the magician, who brings the girl back to life in exchange for his kingdom. At first, the girl refuses to consent to the marriage because the prince raped her. But once she learns that the father of her child is the noble Frayre de Joy, she agrees and the prince becomes the successor to her father as emperor of Gint-Senay (Léglu 2010:102).

In her interpretation of the poem, Catherine Léglu describes how the young prince attributes consent to Sor de Plaser by kissing her a hundred times until her lips move in response, and then exchanging his ring for hers as a promise of betrothal to justify the rape (2010:106–107). She maintains that, throughout the poem, the prince sees signs of the dead girl's active consent. This line from the poem indicates the level of the prince's hallucinations of consent: "And it seemed to him that she was smiling gently at him, and that she was satisfied" (2010:106). "The text," says Léglu, "endorses his forceful reinterpretation of her dead body as a consenting partner with a proverbial expression" containing the girl's name, *Plaser* or pleasure: "Pleasure loves, pleasure desires; thinking brings worry, pleasure guides" (2010:106–107). At the time that this fairytale was written, it was widely held that women could not conceive without an orgasm. Thus, Sleeping Beauty's pregnancy would be proof of her consent.[6] This absurd view has recently reappeared in the political arena after the Republican representative from Missouri, Todd Akin, said in an interview, "'legitimate rape' does not lead to pregnancy. . . . If it's a legitimate rape, the female body has ways to try to shut that whole thing down" (Franke-Ruta 2012).

Léglu discusses another Sleeping Beauty tale, *cantare of Belris*, from fourteenth-century Italy, wherein the girl is sleeping under an enchantment rather than dead. In this tale, Prince Belris is tasked with retrieving a falcon. While out slaying dragons, he has sex with another woman along the way. Eventually, he finds a sleeping queen, whom he rapes, leaving her a note with instructions for the name of the son she just conceived. The birth of the son awakens the sleeping queen and she commands her army to find Belris and makes him marry her. His other mistress kills herself and leaves her own son orphaned. In another version of this medieval tale, believing his daughter Clarisse is cursed, a father locks her in a garden with her governess to protect her. The girl falls ill and the nurse gives her wine to make her well. The girl goes into a drunken stupor and the governess goes off to Mass. A passing prince comes upon her, sees her alone in the garden, and taken by her beauty, he kisses her. Like Frayre de Joy, he interprets the girl's lack of response as consent. Since the girl doesn't resist, he rapes the drunken girl (Léglu 2010:121).

These tales morph into the medieval courtly romantic poem *Perceforest* wherein a princess, Zellandine, falls in love with a prince, Troylus, who must perform courageous feats to win her hand. While he is off on his adventures, she falls into a deep sleep from an enchantment. Upon his return, he rapes her while she is sleeping and impregnates her. He removes the flax from her finger that caused the enchantment and they marry. The question, of course, is why he didn't wake her before having sex with her. In these tales, the fantasy of the sleeping or dead girl not only ensures the lack of resistance to sex but also engenders illusions of consent, and even sexual satisfaction and love, on the part of the unconscious girl. Sex, consent, and satisfaction are all the property of men and their fantasy projections onto incapacitated girls and women. This medieval fantasy of consent is echoed in a remark made by one of the boys involved in the gang rape of an unconscious high school girl in Steubenville (Ohio), who said, "It isn't really rape because you don't know if she wanted to or not" (Ley 2013). The illusion that unconscious girls may want sex, even enjoy it, is still with us. From fairytales to pornography, popular culture is filled with girls and women, unconscious or sleeping, "enjoying" nonconsensual sex. And until we change our fantasies, it is going to be difficult to change our realities.

A PRINCESS IS BEING DRUGGED

Starting with Charles Perrault's (1608–1703) *La Belle au Bois Dormant*, "Sleeping Beauty in the Wood," modern versions of the tale displace the prince's rape of the unconscious girl with the prick from a spindle, followed by a kiss from the prince. In Perrualt's version, and in the Brothers Grimm's *Dornröschen* or "Little Briar Rose," a beautiful princess falls under a sleeping enchantment and is awakened by a kiss from a handsome prince. The issue of consent falls away as an explicit part of the narrative, and the girl wakes up to the man of her dreams, who breaks the spell, and then marries her. With Walt Disney's animated version of the classic fairytale (1959), Sleeping Beauty is named Aurora and the rape from earlier versions is transformed into "true love's kiss." In this familiar version, Aurora is cursed at her christening by an evil fairy named Maleficent: while she will grow up with grace and beauty, on her sixteenth birthday Aurora will prick her finger on a spinning wheel and die. Another fairy modifies the curse so that she doesn't die, but only falls into a deep sleep. Just before Aurora's sixteenth birthday, she meets Prince Philip in the woods, not knowing, of course, that he is a prince. It is love at first sight. Soon after, she pricks her finger and lies sleeping in the castle. Prince Philip must overcome obstacles, most especially Maleficent, to reach Aurora. But after slaying Maleficent, who has transformed herself into a dragon, he wakes Sleeping Beauty with true love's kiss, and they live happily ever after. It is noteworthy that in this version, Sleeping Beauty is acquainted with the prince. He is not a stranger who happens upon the scene. Still, without her consent, he kisses the unconscious girl, whom he loves.

The repression of the rape theme in Sleeping Beauty, specifically in Disney's 1959 film, returns with a vengeance in Disney's recent retelling of the tale, *Maleficent* (2014). In this recent version of Sleeping Beauty, there is a symbolic rape after Maleficent is drugged unconscious by her lover. Indeed, the film revolves around this traumatic moment, which could be interpreted as the rape of a woman intentionally rendered unconscious by drugs administered by her beloved. The film starts with Maleficent's backstory as told in voice-over by a young woman whom we learn at the end of the film is Sleeping Beauty, also known as Aurora. As a winged girl fairy, Maleficent falls in love with a human boy named Stephan. Rather than give her a ring, Stephan proves his love to her by throwing away his only possession in the world, a steel ring that burns Maleficent when it touches her skin. On her sixteenth birthday, Stephan gives her the gift of "true love's kiss." But as he grows up, Stephan becomes more interested in power and fortune than love; eventually he hunts Maleficent (Angelina Jolie) in the hopes of becoming heir to the throne. For the dying king has promised his throne to whoever can kill the winged beast.

Stephan (Sharito Copley) goes back to the enchanted forest, the Moors, land of the fairies, and calls out to Maleficent, who answers. They spend the night together, seemingly rekindling their love. Stephan gives Maleficent something to drink out of a flask, as she lovingly puts her head on his shoulder. Drugged, Maleficent falls into a deep sleep and Stephan pulls out his dagger to kill her. When he looks upon his sleeping beauty, he can't go through with it. Instead, he cuts off her wings and takes them as a prize, as evidence that he "vanquished" Maleficent. When she awakens, wingless and alone, betrayed by her true love, she cries out in anguish. Her loving and trusting personality changes into bitter vengefulness and sorrow. We could say, like most victims of sexual assault, she suffers from post-traumatic stress disorder. The trauma of her symbolic rape drives the rest of the plot.

Unlike other contemporary versions of the Sleeping Beauty / Snow White story that displace the violence of the rape of an unconscious girl onto true love's kiss, Disney's 2014 version shows the symbolic rape of Maleficent. This symbolic rape is also date rape insofar as Stephan tells her he loves her, then drugs her, and violently assaults and dismembers her. Maleficent's "evil" is attributed to her trauma, and her attempts to avenge Stephan's brutal betrayal. When King Stephan and his queen have a baby girl, Maleficent attends the christening uninvited. She curses the girl to grow in grace and beauty until her sixteenth birthday when she will prick her finger on a spinning wheel and die. Under protests from King Stephan and the other fairies, Maleficent amends the curse so that Aurora will not die but rather fall into a deep sleep that can only be awakened by *true love's kiss*, an explicit jab at Stephan's past false promises of true love and true love's kiss. No longer believing in the possibility of true love, Maleficent is confident that she has cursed the girl to sleep forever.

The king entrusts Aurora to three fairies to raise her, away from the castle and away from any spinning wheels. Maleficent watches Aurora grow, and she saves her from the ineptitude of her caregivers, who are too self-absorbed to take care of the child. As a teenager, Aurora (Elle Fanning) says she wants to leave her "aunties" and come to live with Maleficent, whom she calls her "fairy godmother." Touched, Maleficent tries to break her own curse, but can't. As the story goes, just before her sixteenth birthday, Aurora meets Prince Philip in the woods. While they don't declare their love, they are obviously interested in each other. When she tells her aunties that she is leaving them to live in the Moors, they spill the beans about her father, King Stephan, and her home, the castle. Aurora goes to the castle, where Stephan locks her up to prevent the curse from coming true. Alas, in a cursed trance, Aurora finds a spinning wheel, pricks her finger, and falls into a death-like sleep. Hoping that Prince Philip can deliver true love's kiss and break the spell, Maleficent and her trusty familiar, a crow named Diaval, drag the prince to the palace. The three fairy aunties beg him to kiss Aurora. At first, he demurs, saying that he doesn't know her well enough. But he never mentions that she is unconscious, and therefore cannot consent, or that lack of consent might be a reason to think twice about kissing her. Of course, as we've seen in earlier versions of the fairytale, lack of resistance has been interpreted as consent. He cannot deny she is beautiful, or that he wants to kiss her, so eventually he does. But the spell is not broken and Aurora remains asleep.

Lamenting her curse and what she's done to her daughter surrogate, Maleficent asks for Aurora's forgiveness, which she says she does not deserve. She kisses Aurora on the forehead, and sure enough, the princess wakes up. True love's kiss is not delivered by the prince, or by the lover, but rather by the mother, the fairy godmother. The bond between mother and daughter brings Aurora back to life. Aurora goes back to the Moors with Maleficent where presumably they live happily ever after. Because it's Hollywood and Disney, the heterosexual couple must be reunited at the end, and Prince Philip has joined them in the Moors. This is also the case in the popular animated film *Frozen* (2013), where Princess Anna and Kristof end up together, even though Elsa delivers the true love's kiss that awakens her frozen sister Anna. Love between sisters, although stronger than that between lovers, is reinscribed at the end of the film within the heterosexual narrative of prince and princess living happily ever after. So too in *Maleficent,* while true love is that between mother and daughter and not between prince and princess, the prince makes another appearance at the end—although in this case the movie ends with Maleficent flying high above the clouds on her newly attached wings, which were freed by Aurora after she was awoken from the spell.

The film ends with the same voice-over with which it began, telling us that Maleficent is both the hero and villain of the story. The narrative, however, tells a different story, one where King Stephan is the villain, who lies, drugs, and symbolically rapes his "true love" to gain fame and fortune. He dies trying to kill Maleficent. And presumably, the union between Aurora, crowned queen of the Moors by Maleficent, and Prince Philip will unite the two kingdoms of fairies and humans, a union whose true bond has already been forged between fairy godmother Maleficent and her beloved human "daughter" Sleeping Beauty. Although Aurora, Elsa, and Anna are beautiful feminine princesses, shown wearing familiar flowing dresses and long flowing locks, they are extravagant girls insofar as they give priority to their love for the women in their lives over finding or keeping Prince Charming. Indeed, for both Anna and Maleficent, "Prince Charming" turns out to betray them for fame and fortune. Moreover, Elsa and Maleficent reject heterosexual romantic love entirely in favor of love relations with the women in their lives. Love between women is shown as true love, whereas heterosexual love is transitory and deceptive. In this regard, these films may signal some progress in terms of the valuation of relations between women, and suspicions of deceptive princes. Rather than repeating the evil stepmother or stepsister themes so common in fairytales, along with the fantasy of the perfect prince saving the princess from the evil women in her life, these films embrace love between women and debunk the fantasy of the perfect prince who will save the helpless princess.

SLEEPING BEAUTY'S WAKING NIGHTMARE

Although Beatrice "Tris" Prior may not look like a princess in her khaki cargo pants and boy's tank-top undershirt, there are elements of the Sleeping Beauty and Snow White fairytales in Veronica Roth's Young Adult dystopia, *Divergent* books and films (2014 & 2015). Like Sleeping Beauty, Beatrice Prior (Shailene Woodley) undergoes an awakening. Beatrice awakens from her self-sacrificing life as an Abnegation into the violent world of the Dauntless. Like Sleeping Beauty, at the age of sixteen, at the choosing ceremony, Tris pricks herself, spills her blood, and her life is transformed. Like Sleeping Beauty, this is her fate, predetermined by forces greater than herself. Unlike Sleeping Beauty, however, rather than fall asleep when she pricks her finger, Tris wakes up. In *Divergent*, her love interest Four (Theo James) tells her that rather than overpowering her, "fear doesn't shut you down, it wakes you up." The theme of sleeping and waking is common to the *Divergent* series and the Sleeping Beauty and Snow White tales. For example, in *Insurgent*, the second book in the series, the Erudite faction orders an attack on the factionless with whom Tris and Four are hiding out; they shoot little silver balls into everyone to put them to sleep. Tris is knocked out for a few minutes, but wakes up before everyone else because the sleeping potion is not effective on Divergents. While the rest of the kingdom is asleep, Tris is awake. In the Sleeping Beauty tale, when the princess sleeps so does the kingdom. *Divergent* can be read as the awakening of Sleeping Beauty and the liberation of Snow White from her glass coffin.

In the Grimm version of Snow White, the heroine is put into a glass coffin and awakened by the prince's moving the coffin and dislodging the poisonous apple from her throat. In *Divergent*, Tris is repeatedly put into a glass coffin-like box that fills with water. As in other simulations, when she is locked in the glass box, she sees her reflection, realizes it isn't real, and only then can break the glass. Watching Tris easily break the glass simply by tapping on it, Four realizes she is Divergent. Later, Four teaches Tris how to beat the simulation the way a Dauntless would, by finding tools and fighting back, rather than by telling herself that it isn't real, which is how a Divergent overcomes the obstacle and beats the simulation. Tris must hide the fact that she is self-aware, which is evidence of her divergence; she must act like the other Dauntless drones. No one must know she is awake while others sleep. In the book, but not in the film, Jeanine captures Tris and puts her in a real glass coffin identified as such, which fills with water; her mother Natalie Prior (Ashley Judd), rescues her and then sacrifices herself so that Tris can escape (which she does in the film too, but under different circumstances). Unlike many of her recent heroine sisters, Tris's savior is her mother and not always the "prince." Like Katniss in *The Hunger Games*, Tris spends as much time saving her prince as he does saving her. While Tris is strong, fearless, and, in *Insurgent* at least, resembles a prince more than a princess, like other sixteen-year-old girls in recent films, she not only gives as good as she gets, but she gets it good. She is beaten, shot, tortured, bruised, bleeding, groped, and left for dead (fig. 1.1).

FIGURE 1.1 Tris (Shailene Woodley) bloodied and beaten unconscious in the first round of Dauntless trials.

Just as Sleeping Beauty, and her fairytale twin Snow White, are both left for dead after being poisoned and cursed by an evil sadistic queen, Tris is the target of a cold and heartless "white witch," Jeanine, the head of Erudite. Like Snow White and Sleeping Beauty, Tris has her prince in Four, a prince who plays an essential part in her awakening from the Abnegation girl she once was. If *Divergent* can be read as an updated Sleeping Beauty, however, it is the story of a girl's awakening into her most violent impulses and the violence of the world around her, a world that she navigates only with help from her mother and her prince. Still interested in true love and true love's kiss, our contemporary Sleeping Beauty is neither sleeping nor beautiful but rather more like the sentinel staying awake to protect the kingdom with her true grit, spurred on by anger rather than love. Defying her Abnegation upbringing, Tris dares to look into the "mirror, mirror on the wall" and her reflection reminds her of what is real and what is illusion. This "princess" can tell reality from a fairytale.

More importantly, if the classic myth of Sleeping Beauty is a tale of rape, the film version of *Divergent* is no exception. In the context of thinking about the Sleeping Beauty tale as one of rape, rape as part of the story of a girl's coming-of-age, and of date rape in particular, let's turn to the controversial rape scene in the film version of *Divergent*. In the first film, in a drug-induced simulation of her "fearscape," our heroine Tris Prior has successfully faced her deepest fears. She has fought off an attack of crows reminiscent of Hitchcock's *The Birds*, escaped being burned at the stake, and freed herself from a glass box filled with water.[7] After Tris fights off the crows and overcomes the other obstacles in the simulation, her boyfriend Four takes her into his room and kisses her. Then he tries to lift her shirt and she pushes his hand away. Four shoves Tris onto the bed and asks, "Aren't you dauntless?" suggesting that if she were, she wouldn't be afraid of his advances. She resists and says "no." In spite of her protests, Four forces himself on her. The screen fills with his face moving toward her (and the audience), reminiscent of the controversial rape scene in Hitchcock's *Marnie*

FIGURE 1.2   Four (Theo James) sexually assaulting Tris in her "fearscape" in *Divergent* (2014), directed by Neil Burger.

where Sean Connery's face fills the screen as his character, Mark, forces himself on Marnie. Unlike Marnie, Tris fights off Four with a kick to the groin.

At this point, the audience realizes it has been a simulation. The film continues with more simulations within simulations,

FIGURE 1.3   Four's assault from Tris's perspective.

including Four again congratulating an embarrassed Tris, whose rape fantasy-phobia has just been played on big screens for all to see. Reminiscent of images of raped and groped unconscious or sleeping girls circulating on social media, Tris's near-rape is recorded and watched by an audience. Attempted rape as a spectator sport.

Although Four doesn't succeed in raping her, this scene is telling. One of Tris's deepest fears, part of her "fearscape," displayed for all to see, is that her new boyfriend will force her to have sex against her will. She is afraid that her boyfriend might rape her. This is not a fear of rape in general, or a fear of men, but rather a fear of "date rape." And while it is "just" a hallucination and she successfully stops him, the scene makes manifest a deep-seated fear that hits close to home—namely, that like Tris, girls are at risk of being drugged, incapacitated, and raped by those closest to them. After all, Tris is served the serum that induces the simulation in a large shot glass; the first test administrator tells her "bottoms up," an obvious nod to drinking shots and the effects of alcohol. Tris is drugged, and then sexually assaulted in the simulation, which is reproduced on computer screens and watched by a rapt audience of spectators. For the film audience, duped into first believing that Four's sexual assault is real and not part of the simulation, Tris has to fight off unwanted sexual advances from the person closest to her.

Notably, the attempted rape scene is not in the book, but was added for dramatic effect to the film. This scene sparked debates in the blogosphere over whether or not *Divergent* is a feminist film, and whether it shows a young woman doing the right thing in fighting back, or is completely unrealistic since it's unlikely that a small girl like Tris could overpower the muscle-bound Four. Some praised the film for its representation of a strong girl who insists that "no means no" (Thomas 2014), while others argued that it sends the message that girls should be able to fight and overpower their attackers, and if they can't then they are to blame (Smith 2014). Most defended Four, since it was a hallucination after all, and the "real" Four "would never do something like that." The attempted rape may have been a simulation, but Tris's fear was real. What is more interesting, though, is that lots of people, seemingly both men and women, commented on a YouTube clip of this scene that they watched this particular scene over and over again, some saying that it was "hot," and one saying that it made him want to "fuck her hard."[8] The scene is shot in soft-focus, suggesting hallucination, but also suggesting romance. And while within the narrative of the film, the attempted rape is from Tris's fearscape (her deepest fears), it plays as a sexual fantasy. Whether desire or fear, the scene is created from Tris's imagination. Of course, given the statistics on acquaintance and date rape, we could read this fear as a realistic fear of violent forced sex by someone known, or even loved. For teenage girls and young women coming-of-age in hookup and party rape culture, this fear is all too real.

It is also crucial to note that the simulated attempted rape scene is not the only scene in which Four attacks Tris. Under the influence of mind-altering drugs, the "real" Four beats Tris and almost kills her when he is held at the Erudite compound. Up until this point, the drugs administered by Erudite provoke fear responses to the subject's deepest fears. This should make us wonder why

FIGURE 1.4 Four attacking Tris in *Divergent*.

FIGURE 1.5   Under the influence of drugs, Four chokes Tris.

Four is afraid of Tris. At the climax of the scene, he chokes her
and holds a gun to her head, an image we've seen before in his fear
landscape when he is ordered to kill an innocent girl. In that earlier
scene, Tris had accompanied him into his fear landscape where he
told her that he can only pull the trigger if he looks away.

At one point in his hallucination, the innocent stranger with the
gun to her head is replaced by Tris, suggesting that if Four is not
afraid of Tris, he is afraid of killing her. In the Erudite lab, when
Four attacks Tris and *really* puts the gun to her head, she repeatedly says, "It's me, it's me. I love you," and forces him to look at
her. Once he looks at her, he comes to and turns the gun on his
captors, saving both himself and Tris.

Regardless of whether or not Four intended to attack Tris, or
even knew he was beating her, the viewer watches a girl being
beaten. Regardless of whether or not Four is real or part of a simulation, the viewer watches him try to rape Tris. *Divergent* is filled
with scenes of girls being beaten. Of course, boys are being beaten
too. But it is the girl-on-girl violence, and especially the boy-on-girl
violence, that makes the film edgy. Under the pretext of tough girls

holding their own, fighting back, and even initiating violence, we get to watch girls being beaten by boys and almost raped. Under the pretext of girl power and feminist empowerment, we watch girl-on-girl violence, as if to prove that violence is no longer just the purview of men. And when women fight, especially girl-on-girl, it's seen as sexy.

Another example of brutal violence toward girls is in the films *Kick-Ass* and *Kick-Ass 2*. In the first film, twelve-year-old Hit Girl is beaten unconscious by an adult male mafia thug. This scene near the end of *Kick-Ass* is hard to watch. Hit Girl fights the head of the mob, a big brutal man, who beats this prepubescent girl until she is lying bleeding, moaning, and eventually unconscious, on a table. It is shocking to see a little girl beaten so viciously in a mainstream blockbuster film. Perhaps more so because this scene was shot like any other in the film and her abuse is shown in the same light as that of gangster-on-gangster violence.

While the images of young girls being beaten may be staged and shot in the same ways as villains fighting, the sounds of girls

FIGURE 1.6 Twelve-year-old Hit Girl (Chloë Grace Moretz) choked by mob boss in *Kick-Ass* (2010), directed by Matthew Vaughn.

FIGURE 1.7 Hit Girl beaten and bloodied.

crying, moaning, or whimpering are not the same as men's. The brutal scene in which tiny Hit Girl is beaten bloody and left unconscious is unsettling not only because her attacker is literally twice her size, but also because the sobs of a little girl are not the same as the cries of an adult man. In that moment when she starts to

FIGURE 1.8 Hit Girl unconscious and left for dead.

cry, we are reminded that she is a little girl and not just a trained assassin. Unlike the sixteen-year-old heroines in most of the other films I've discussed, within the narrative of this film she is only twelve years old. Indeed, the actress playing Hit Girl, Chloë Grace Moretz, was only eleven at the time of filming, while our other tough girls are actually older than their characters. For example, Jennifer Lawrence was twenty-two when she first played sixteen-year-old Katniss Everdeen in *The Hunger Games*.

The climax of *Kick-Ass 2* (2013) is a brutal fight between a now teenage Hit Girl and Mother Russia (a member of the "Mega-Cunts" gang recruited by the villain "Motherfucker") in which again Hit Girl is almost killed before she finally turns the tables on her opponent and cuts Mother Russia to death with shards of glass. In an interview, the young actress Chloë Grace Moretz, who plays Hit Girl/Mindy, says she was looking for an "Angelina Jolie type" part that showed a strong female character and empowered girls. Yet, again, in the name of girl power, we watch girls being brutally beaten, and brutalizing each other. Hit Girl may be a foul-mouthed assassin, but she's still just a little girl. Have these little girls grown up and entered the man's world of violence as equals? Are they equal-opportunity killers? Or are these films justifications for taking pleasure in the abuse of girls?

Another vicious beating scene is *Winter's Bone* (2010) extremely violent battering of sixteen-year-old Ree Dolly (Jennifer Law-rence), who is badly injured. Hers is an exceptionally violent beating that leaves her nearly dead.

While Ree doesn't "give as good as she gets," her teenage filmic sisters, Hanna, Katniss, Bella, and Tris, can hold their own with the worst villains. Hanna and Katniss are particularly well served by their hunting skills, taught to them by their fathers. Yet regardless of their toughness and skills—or maybe because of them—all of these girls are shown beating and being beaten. They carry weapons (or in Bella's case, her super newborn vampire strength is her weapon), guns and arrows. These hot girls are packing heat. Tris, Hit Girl, and Hanna carry huge guns, and they aren't afraid to use

FIGURE 1.9 Ree Dolly (Jennifer Lawrence) beaten in *Winter's Bone* (2010), directed by Debra Granik.

them. Tris, Katniss, and Bella are ready to fight for survival and for their families. Yet in some scenes it is difficult to watch these young girls suffering abuse at the hands of others, especially adult men.

Like *Twilight* and *The Hunger Games*, *Divergent* shows us teenagers attacking and killing each other: equal-opportunity beatings, indiscriminate of gender. These films answer a call for empowered girls by giving us violent girls who beat and get beaten. Yet these films also seem to satisfy a perverse desire to see girls abused and beaten as punishment for becoming strong and independent. In other words, within the logic of these fantasies, because girls give as good as they get, they deserve to be punished. The brutal violence against girls in these films suggests a response to feminists' calls for strong female characters by giving us tough girls, and then beating the shit out of them. Within the patriarchal imagination, these young upstarts deserve to be beaten. They have it coming. And it is titillating to watch, as evidenced by the popularity of these films. Recall that online viewers repeatedly replay the scene of Four lifting Tris's shirt and pushing her onto his bed—his face filling the screen as he forces himself on her, and she fights him off—because they find it "hot." In these blockbusters, hot girls take heat for standing up for themselves.

In these the coming-of-age stories about sixteen-year-olds, abuse and violence are linked with the awakening of sexual desires. For our teenaged protagonists, the transition into womanhood is marked by violence, and their first sexual desires are surrounded by danger. For example, Hanna's first kiss is just an interlude in her chasing and being chased by evil CIA operatives. Katniss's first kiss takes place in the Hunger Games with danger on all sides as she fights for her life. Tris is fighting for her life in Dauntless training when she first kisses Four; and obviously she is afraid of him, as evidenced by the simulation in which she hallucinates his attempting to rape her. Bella's sexual desires for Edward constantly put her in danger, not just from the forces of evil vampires or the Volturi (the vampire police that condemn the union) but also from Edward himself; sex with Edward while she is still human could kill her and leaves her bruised and battered; and childbirth with his human-vampire hybrid baby does kill her.[9] In *Kick-Ass 2*, Hit Girl, whose real name is Mindy, is set up on her first date, taken to the forest, and left there. She compares the encounter to the first time "Big Daddy" sent her into a crack den with only a penknife. At the end of the film, she initiates her first kiss and then threatens the boy to be nice or she'll rip his ass through his mouth. Finally, think of Carrie (*Carrie* 1976, 2013), whose first date ends with a bloody massacre.

Although Lisbeth Salander in *The Girl with the Dragon Tattoo* is older than her filmic teenage sisters, she not only is still considered "a girl," as the title suggests, but also is beaten, abused, and violently raped in the course of both the Swedish and American film adaptations of the book. As film critics A. O. Scott and Manohla Dargis argue: "It is in the nature of the moving image to give pleasure, and in the nature of film audiences—consciously or not, admittedly or not—to find pleasure in what they see. So in depicting Salander's rape by her guardian in the graphic way he did, the director, Niels Arden Oplev, ran the risk of aestheticizing, glamorizing and eroticizing it. . . . The risk is not dissolved but rather compounded when the answering, avenging violence is staged and shot in almost exactly

FIGURE 1.10 Lisbeth Salander (Noomi Rapace) manhandled by her guardian before he sexually assaults and rapes her in *The Girl with the Dragon Tattoo* (2009), directed by Niels Arden Oplev.

the same kind of gruesome detail, since the audience knows it is supposed to enjoy that" (2011). (See figure 1.10.)

Arguably, the Hollywood version directed by David Fincher is even more problematic in that it sensationalizes Lisbeth's rape by Bjurman and shows it in lurid detail that is lacking in the equally graphic revenge scene. As Scott puts it, "Mr. Fincher approaches it [sexual violence] with queasy, teasing sensationalism. Lisbeth's dealings with Bjurman include a vicious rape and a correspondingly brutal act of revenge, and there is something prurient and salacious about the way the initial assault is filmed. The vengeance, while graphic, is visually more circumspect" (Scott 2011). As in the earlier films discussed, violence toward girls and women is filmed in ways that make it aesthetically pleasing. By doing so, these films not only aestheticize and eroticize violence toward girls and women, and sexual assault, but also normalize it and anesthetize us to its effects.

Some of these films trade on rape fantasies that seemingly sell. Scott and Dargis argue that *Sucker Punch* (2011), which also features tough girls fighting with men, "gains in sleaziness by coyly keeping its rape fantasies within PG-13 limits and fairly quivering with ecstasy as it contemplates scenes of female victimization" (2011). In *Sucker Punch*, Babydoll (Emily Browning) is a teenage girl trying to escape a mental institution where her stepfather has wrongly imprisoned her; she uses her fantasy life to cope with the trauma of her abusive stepfather and abusive orderlies, and to plan her escape from the hospital before her scheduled lobotomy. In sum, there is a sensational titillating attention paid to violence toward girls and young women in these films. Camera angles, lingering shots on body parts, and soft-focus photography work to aestheticize violence toward girls and women, and to anesthetize us to it. Our fascination with girls with guns signals anxieties about the pubescent sexual desires of girls. With their big guns and arrows, these are phallic virgins packing heat. Is it the combination of innocence and budding womanhood that makes these teenage girls so attractive? And is "the girl is being beaten" fantasy a response to this heady combination? Within these fantasies, is abuse or punishment seemingly warranted by the fact that these girls excite sexual desires in men, boys, and the audience?

Scott and Dargis's analysis of *The Girl with the Dragon Tattoo* and *Hanna* in various ways applies to all of these films: "what fuels these fantasies is also a deep anxiety—an unstable compound of confusion, fascination, panic and denial—about female sexuality, especially the sexual power and vulnerability of girls and young women" (2011). These coming-of-age stories about girls kicking ass and getting their asses kicked while giving or receiving their first kiss not only serve as cautionary fairytales warning girls of the dangers of womanhood but also as titillating fantasies of feminine sexuality as both dangerous and fascinating. The combination of sexual power and vulnerable innocence of girls is a heady blend at the theater. In the case of our pubescent and prepubescent heroines, they may not be sex objects in the way that their adult women counterparts are (think of Angelina Jolie's Lara Croft), but that makes them all the more fascinating. Their tomboy tendencies make them all the more appealing. And their pubescent transitional status between girls and women make them a type of hybrid creature whose allure provokes anxiety.

These teenaged heroines are strong and they wield weapons. At the same time, they are innocent, even naïve (think of Hanna). There is still something open-ended about their power and their innocence as they make their way into womanhood. There is a still a question of whether or not they will follow the traditional path circumscribed for women, namely marriage and family. This in-between space is exciting, even sexy, a space full of promise.[10] It is also a dangerous space for these girls. They face violence from all sides, even from those closest to them. What happens during their transition to womanhood determines whether or not girls will break free of patriarchal stereotypes and restrictions and go their own ways. It is here that the road forks and they can either break out on their own like Hanna, or embrace traditional values of marriage and family like Bella. And who is to say which is the more dangerous? It seems that if the most popular films, *The Hunger Games* and *Twilight*, are any indication, marriage and family are the safer bets. (We will see if *The Hunger Game* sequels have Katniss marry Peeta and give birth to two children, a boy and a girl, as she does in the epilogue to the book trilogy.) Regardless, the path to womanhood for these girls is filled with beatings, battery, abuse, and sometimes sexual assault. In Bella's case, even her "normal" sex life with her vampire husband is violent and dangerous. And with Bella Swan's soft-porn alter ego Anastasia Steel in the runaway best seller, *Fifty Shades of Grey*, sexual violence has made a comeback as the stuff of fairytales.

FIFTY SHADES OF CONSENT

Arguably, the popularity of *The Girl with the Dragon Tattoo* series along with *Fifty Shades of Grey*, in which the female protagonist is subjected to her lover's sadistic sexual tendencies and learns to enjoy them, is evidence of the eroticization of sexual violence. Violent sex has gone mainstream with the popularity of the *Fifty Shades of Grey* book trilogy and film. The first book in the series has sold more copies than any other novel in history and rivals the Bible in worldwide sales. *Fifty Shades* delivers violent and kinky sex wrapped up in a familiar romance, what one critic calls "Cinderella Porn" (Travers 2015). Anastasia Steele meets handsome billionaire Christian Grey, falls in love, and tries to save him from his traumatic past and his current obsession with violent sex. Eventually, becoming a husband and father cures him of his kinky sexual preferences. Many commentators have criticized *Fifty Shades of Grey* for suggesting that BDSM (Bondage, Dominance, Sadism, and Masochism) is pathological and needs to be cured.[11] Some of these critics also point out that the consent and mutual sexual pleasure crucial to the BDSM community is missing from, or misrepresented in, *Fifty Shades* (Barker 2013; Green 2015; Hasty 2015). They claim that practitioners of BDSM follow strict rules for the benefit of safe, mutually satisfying sex, rules that are broken or undermined in *Fifty Shades*.

In a series that ultimately turns around nonconsensual sex acts forced on Ana by Christian through either coercion or threats, it may be surprising that consent is a main theme of *Fifty Shades*. Christian insists that before they have sex, Anastasia must sign a contract agreeing to be his submissive. This would mean he controls not only their sex but also other aspects of her life, including what she eats and what she wears. It also would mean that he gets to hit her, tie her up, blindfold her, and put things into her body, whenever he wants. Ana refuses to sign the contract. But that doesn't stop Christian from controlling their sex, what she eats, what she wears, what car she drives, and other aspects of her life. Even though he doesn't have written consent, Christian hits Ana, ties her up, blindfolds her, and puts things into her body. He does this, more or less, with Ana's verbal consent, although (in the books at least) we know Ana is doing it just to please him and not because she wants it; to the contrary, she doesn't. In the film, Ana is shown saying, "Yes please," when Christian asks to tie her up. Interviews with the makers of the film, including the actors, always stress that the violent sex between Christian and Ana is consensual. The film emphasizes the theme of consent from the novels, with at least four conversations about the contract and the importance of consent.

Still, Ana never signs the contract. She never gives her written consent. And it is her refusal that continues to drive the plot. The film gets steamy when a lusty and impatient Christian says, "Fuck the paperwork," and passionately kisses Ana in an elevator, breaking his own rules (in the novel he says "screw the paperwork"). Control-freak Christian loses control. This is Ana's power over him. This is why the books and the film are hot. This is also why *Fifty Shades* is a love story. A virgin falls for a sadist and he falls for her, but sex is what might come between them, so to speak. Ana is special and we know Christian loves her because he can't control himself around her. A man of integrity, a man in control, a man who never breaks his own rules, loses himself completely over Ana. And this is proof of his love. In the end, this is also his cure. When he submits to Ana, the old Christian is lost and the new loving husband and father is born.

Here, we see how *Fifty Shades* began as fan fiction for *Twilight*, which is also a story of a high-minded man (or in this case, eternal boy), Edward the vampire, struggling to control himself and his natural urges when he is around Bella. In fact, all of the vampires have a hard time controlling themselves around Bella because she is constantly cutting herself and bleeding. Her sweet blood is almost irresistible. Like Ana in *Fifty Shades*, Bella pushes Edward to the edge of his control. Even more than in *Fifty Shades*, in *Twilight* the virgin Bella begs for sex with Edward. He refuses because he could very well kill her by accident during sex, especially if he lost control. On their wedding day, Bella's best friend Jacob warns her that sex with Edward while she is still human will kill her. She wants it anyway. In fact, on their honeymoon, she insists that Edward have sex with her. The force of sex with Edward breaks the bed and leaves her badly bruised. Yet, she begs for more.

Throughout the *Twilight* books and films, Bella courts danger at every turn. She keeps Edward and Jacob on high alert, ready to save her at any time. She says she trusts Edward not to lose control, and yet she thrives on making him lose control. Again, in the terms of *Twilight*, as in *Fifty Shades*, it is Edward's loss of control that proves his love. He is overpowered by his love for Bella. Edward may be a nearly all-powerful, 100-year-old vampire with the ability to read minds, but a teenage girl overpowers him through love. Christian may be a powerful, rich businessman who has always gotten his way, but a college girl overpowers him through love. As I've argued elsewhere, "Bella wants risky sex almost as much as she wants to be changed into a vampire, in other words, almost as much as she wants death itself. . . . She wants to keep Edward on the edge of his ability to control his desires, and only then can she satisfy hers. . . . Within the world of *Twilight* feminine sexuality is driven by risky, even masochistic, behaviors that repeatedly leave Bella bruised, bleeding, and on the edge of death" (Oliver 2012).

Both Bella and Ana bring out something uncontrollable in their boyfriends. Both push the limits of these controlling men's ability to control themselves. And both stories value this loss of control as a sign of love. But it is also this loss of control that makes sex dangerous. Bella is badly hurt during sex with Edward. And Ana is hurt during sex with Christian. While Bella is asking for more dangerous sex, however, Ana is only reluctantly agreeing to submit to painful sexual activities requested by Christian against her better judgment because she is afraid of losing him and doesn't want to appear weak. Although Ana (most of the time) gives verbal consent, she alternates between sexual ecstasy and unwanted pain and humiliation. Both girls are stalked by their boyfriends, who invade their private space, spy on them, and tell them what to do. Bella awakens to Edward passionately watching her sleep, just barely able to control his urges to turn her into another Sleeping Beauty victim of unconscious date rape.

In what Nancy Bauer calls the logic of the "pornutopia" where all women enjoy violent sex and ask for more, Bella gets off on being battered and bruised and comes back for more (Bauer 2015). The same goes for Ana. In terms of sexual pleasure, *Fifty Shades* is part of the "pornutopia." Without asking, or any experimentation, Christian knows exactly how to send Ana into sexual ecstasy, in spite of herself. Moreover, he does so by exercising his own desires; and in the pornutopia, acting on one's own sexual desires always satisfies the recipient, no matter what they say or how they feel about these sexual activities. Christian claims to know Ana's desires better than she does. In one scene in the film, he says, "You want to leave? Your body tells me something different." Rather than listening to what she says, he "reads" her body, which tells him that her "no" really means "yes." In the pornutopia, consent is irrelevant to sexual pleasure. Or perhaps consent is not irrelevant, but precisely the focal point. *Lack of consent is hot.*

Perhaps the *Fifty Shades* fantasy of a girl doing things she doesn't really want in order to keep her guy is not far from the reality of many girls in hookup culture. Studying hookup culture on college campuses, sociologist Kathleen Bogle found that girls are pressured to go further than they'd like in hopes that the hookup will turn into a relationship (2008). Of course, this is a danger of dating too. Bogle also found that although attitudes toward casual sex, especially sex initiated by women, have changed, the double standard for men and women has not. Men are "players" if they have a lot of sex, whereas women are still "sluts" (2008:179). While hookups can mean anything from kisses to intercourse, Bogle's research shows that misperceptions and expectations can lead hookups to become risky situations, bordering on rape (2008:92). For example, she transcribes an interview with one fraternity boy who told her a really "funny" story about having sex with a girl who was so drunk she couldn't walk and threw up on him during intercourse. He and his friends cleaned her up, and they started "going at it" again (2008:91). From the outside, this "funny" story is the ugly truth about party rape and illusions of consent that take us back to the Middle Ages.

In *Fifty Shades*, lack of consent turns this story from kinky sex into a love story. Lack of consent is crucial to Christian's falling in love and losing control. His passion is at odds with the talk of consent and the contract. Ana's refusal to sign and consent is more of a "turn-on" to him than his BDSM, especially emotionally. The consent contract is the antithesis of spontaneous passionate sex. It is the enemy of love, marriage, and family. So instead of a sex contract, Christian gets more than he bargained for, a marriage contract, which is why this tale of hot sex is really a familiar story of love, marriage, and baby. It is clearer in the book than in the movie that Ana does not want violent painful sex, even though she consents. Her verbal consent has nothing to do with wanting this kind of sex, but rather with wanting Christian to want her. In the book, the reader is privy to Ana's thoughts, which often contradict her actions.[12] We see her struggle to be the woman that Christian wants even though she wants something very different, something he claims he cannot give her. It is clear that the consent she gives is undermined by her own thoughts and desires to the contrary. Although he doesn't physically force her against her will, his controlling personality combined with her love for him and fears of losing him—that is to say, her own insecurities—lead her to consent to things she doesn't want. This type of weak consent must be distinguished from the strong consent many commentators have argued is part and parcel of BDSM. For that matter, Ana's reluctant consent to rough sex with Christian should be distinguished from unambiguous affirmative consent.

There are scenes in the book and the film, particularly the last scene, where Ana makes it very clear to Christian that she doesn't like what he is doing and doesn't want to be the object of his violent pleasures. For example, there is a passage in *Fifty Shades of Grey* where Ana hesitantly submits to a spanking because she has rolled her eyes at Christian and he'd threatened to spank her and "fuck her hard" if she rolled her eyes again. She reminds him that she hasn't signed the contract. He responds that he's a man of his word and he spanks her. The reader knows that she does not want to submit. Her thoughts also tell us that she knows that if she doesn't, Christian will leave her. Afterwards, she is upset that a man has hit her, and supposedly in the name of love. Here, she does not consent; and she reminds him that she has not consented. But in the name of his "integrity" and only partly tongue-in-cheek, he insists on carrying out her punishment. Christian gets off on punishing Ana. He also likes to reward her with expensive gifts in exchange for her submission. Both book and film end with Ana leaving Christian's Red Room after he spanks her hard. She is obviously hurt and runs away crying, leaving behind some of his expensive gifts. This doesn't seem like the behavior of someone enjoying pain or asking to be hit. Regardless of whether or not she gave her verbal consent, she didn't want to be hit and she didn't like it. Moreover, Christian knew that she wouldn't like it, but did it anyway. Like Christian, consent in *Fifty Shades of Grey* is "fifty shades of fucked up."

Ana is the stereotypical helpless, passive woman without any desires of her own. Christian is the stereotypical active man controlling the woman's desires. In this regard, as Megan Barker argues, "*Fifty Shades* reflects broader heteronormative understandings of consent whereby men initiate and women comply or resist" within a liberal notion of individual choice that ignores power differentials, in this case both in terms of gender and class (Barker 2013). Wrapping non-normative sex in the familiar tale of Beauty and the Beast, whereby the virginal innocent girl redeems the traumatized man to transform him into the man of her dreams, we get the fantasy of transgression neatly contained within an easily consumable package with plenty of product spinoffs.[13] Women's choice, sexual freedom, and empowerment are part of the allure of the fantasy, which, it turns out, is really a story of submission, marriage, and reproduction. Women's choice is elided by the fantasy of consent, what Angelika Tsaros calls "consensual non-consent," in a situation where gender and class power dynamics have already pulled the rug out from under sexual empowerment (2013).

The role of consent—or lack thereof—in *Fifty Shades* throws light on the thorny issue of intoxicated consent on college campuses where drugs and alcohol blur the lines of consent (Warshaw 1994).[14] In sum, in *Fifty Shades*, the woman is the submissive and the man the dominant; the woman's consent is (supposedly) something that she freely gives; the woman can consent to what she does not want or desire; consent is a substitute for desire insofar as the woman consents to violent sex but never asks for it; the woman gives (supposedly) her consent for the man to do things to her body and not the other way around; finally, in sex, the man (as dominant) is the actor or agent and the woman (as submissive) is the acted upon or object. Thus, the woman's only active contribution to violent sex is her consent (and her pornuptoic pleasure, which is merely a reaction to the man's sexual prowess). Yet what counts as consent in *Fifty Shades* is ambiguous. This ambiguity perpetuates the dangerous idea that "no means yes," which has become a rallying cry for some fraternities that pride themselves on "bagging" girls using alcohol or drugs and then posting pictures of their prey on the Internet.[15]

Recently on many college campuses (and in some state statutes), rape has been downgraded to "nonconsensual sex." At the same time, we see an increasing valorization of lack of consent. Within some parts of mainstream culture, nonconsensual sex is valued more than consensual sex. The use of cellphone cameras to take pictures of unconscious girls without their consent, and then post those photos on social media, is further evidence of the value placed on lack of consent. Indeed, what is known as the "creepshot," taking pictures of girls and women without their knowledge, is valued precisely because of the lack of consent. Lack of consent is what makes the pictures "candid" rather than posed. Furthermore, as a sign that easy access to online pornography has penetrated mainstream culture, fraternity boys at Ivy League schools chant about necrophilia and high school boys refer to the unconscious victims of sexual abuse as "dead girls." Fraternities host porno-themed costume parties, such as "Dirty Doctors and Naughty Nurses, Mains and Millionaires, Superheroes and Supersluts, Sex and Execs, Horny Housewives and Randy Handy-men" (Freitas 2013:81). "These are the kind of role-play pairings regularly found in porn—but they are also the role-plays typically placed out live at college parties today" (Freitas 2013:81). Some college men take women's sexy attire as an invitation to sex (Bogle 2008; Freitas 2013). As we have seen, with *Fifty Shades of Grey*, BDSM and pornography have gone mainstream.[16] But they've done so in a culture that valorizes a woman's lack of consent, even lack of consciousness, in what some have called *rape culture* (Buchwald et al. 2005). Of course, as we will see in the conclusion, women are fighting back. Activists are making the topic of campus rape an issue in mainstream national media. Educational institutions have also been forced to deal with the issue of sexual assault on campus.

2

RAPE AS SPECTATOR SPORT
AND CREEPSHOT ENTERTAINMENT

IN AN OFFICIAL TRAILER FOR the film *Pitch Perfect 2* (2015), Rebel Wilson's character "Fat Amy" is shown dancing at a campus party when the boy she is dancing with asks if she wants to have sex later. She says "no," but then gives him a suggestive wink. He looks confused and asks whether that means no or yes since she said "no," but then winked. She responds "absolutely not," and then winks again, suggesting that she doesn't mean what she said. What message does this send? When girls say "no," they really mean "yes"? Certainly, Amy's "no" is open for interpretation. In 2010 at Yale, fraternity brothers marched around the freshman dorms chanting "No means yes, yes means anal." Their interpretation of "no" and "yes" is clear. In this chapter, I argue that lack of consent is valorized within popular culture to the point that sexual assault has become a spectator sport and creepshot entertainment on social media. Indeed, the valorization of nonconsensual sex has reached the extreme where sex with unconscious girls, especially accompanied by photographs as trophies, has become a goal of some boys and men.

I trace this valorization of lack of consent back to the four-teenth-century Sleeping Beauty myth, on the one hand, and link it to pornographic fantasies of necrophilia and rape, on the other. I discuss the specific harms of "party rape" to sexual assault victims who are unconscious at the time and discover the violation of their bodies through photographs on social media. I consider how recording rather than reporting may become a new standard for prosecuting rape cases. Finally, I suggest that social media was created for and by men who denigrate women. In conclusion, I consider how social media changes the way in which we conceive of, and view, sexual assault, its harms and prosecution.

The Yale chant suggests that anal sex is the most valuable because it is the most transgressive. Recent highly publicized cases of groups of boys anally gang-raping unconscious girls suggests that these girls function as sex objects exchanged between men within a circuit of their own hypermasculinized homoerotic desires. Anal gang rape is a way to further treat nonconsenting women like objects. One fraternity member interviewed in the documentary *The Hunting Ground* said anal sex was considered the biggest trophy when frat brothers "compared" conquests at his frat house (2015). Recall the gentleman spy in *Kingsman: The Secret Service* (2015) who is rewarded for saving the world with the princess offering him anal sex.

The Yale case is not an isolated incident. Consider a chant used at St. Mary's University in Halifax to welcome new students: "SMU boys, we like them young. Y is for your sister, O is for oh so tight, U is for underage, N is for no consent, G is for grab that ass" (Williams 2013). Or consider a fraternity suspended from Texas Tech for flying a banner that read "No Means Yes" (Schwarz 2015). In 2013, another frat was suspended at Georgia Tech for distributing an email with the subject line "Luring your *rapebait*," which ended, "I want to see everyone succeed at the next couple parties" (Schwarz 2015). And in 2014 at William and Mary, fraternity members sent around an email message, "never mind the extremities that surround it, the 99% of horrendously illogical bullshit that makes up the modern woman, consider only the 1%, the snatch" (McCarthy 2014). The list goes on. These examples suggest an aggressive campaign on the part of some fraternities to insist that "no" means "yes," and consent is not only irrelevant but also undesired. In the St. Mary's chant, the lack of consent is openly valued, "N is for no consent." Actively seeking sex without consent, sometimes even admitting it is rape, turns them on. Whatever their actual desires, these college men are *saying* that they want nonconsensual sex. In fraternity culture, it seems their manhood and masculinity is dependent upon at least *saying*—or chanting—that they want forced sex, or sex with unconscious girls, if not also acting on it.[1]

"NO MEANS YES" AND NONCONSENUSAL SEX

Several studies have shown that many sexual predators buy into the pornutopic fantasy that women enjoy being raped. One study concludes, "rapists, or men identified as unusually likely to rape, are characterized by the belief that rape is not averse to women—that, in fact, women desire and enjoy it" (Hamilton & Yee 1990:112). Clinical reports and interviews with convicted rapists indicate that many rapists "perceive their victims as deriving pleasure from the assault" (Hamilton & Yee 1990:112).[2] Studies of pornography have shown that rape porno is arousing when the woman is shown as aroused by the attack (Hamilton & Yee 1990:113). As we have seen, this fantasy is as old as the legend of Sleeping Beauty aroused while unconscious by the pressure from her rapist's lips.

Young men's attitudes toward consent are formed by exposure to pornography, especially the easily accessed Internet porn, in which rape victims are depicted as enjoying sexual assault. One psychologist says, "The problem for some men who watch large amounts of porn is, as time goes by, they need more stimulation and aggressive porn in order to get aroused. . . . Internet porn has simply become so much a part of society that they don't view themselves as 'hard core' users" (Cuthbertson 2015). In the world of pornography, the desires of the aggressor turn out to be the secret desires of the victim, whether or not she originally says "no." In the words of Nancy Bauer, "Serendipitously, as it always turns out, to gratify yourself sexually by imposing your desires on another person is automatically to gratify that person as well. . . . In the pornutopia, autonomy takes the form of exploring and acting on your sexual desires when and in whatever way you like. . . . When Daddy fucks Becky, she doesn't experience it as rape. She comes" (Bauer 2015:5). Of course, within the pornutopia, the agents are men, who force their desires on women; and the fantasy is that women enjoy it, that "no" really does mean "yes, yes, yes."

This is the *generous* interpretation of the "No Means Yes" campaign on college campuses—namely, that these college boys and men really believe that girls and women want to be raped. Perhaps fraternity brothers or college athletes who are prone to sexual assault have bought into the pornutopia and at some level really believe that "no" means "yes." They have watched enough pornography to be convinced by the fantasy that whatever a woman says, and whether or not she is conscious, she enjoys it. For within the pornutopia, women enjoy violent sex, even abuse. If it turns him on, then within the logic of the pornutopia, it turns her on too. Like the prince in Sleeping Beauty, these sexual predators imagine that their victim's lips are moving in ecstasy. This pornutopic fantasy of mutual satisfaction becomes a justification for acting on their violent desires. It is especially troubling that pornutopic ideas of sex are becoming mainstream thanks to widespread use of easily available pornography. For many boys, pornography provides their first sexual experiences, which may shape future encounters with women and make sex less about intimacy and communication and more of a "one-way street."

The less generous interpretation is that they get off on debasing women, especially through "nonconsensual sex"—what used to be called "rape." Slogans such as "No Means Yes" and "N is for no consent" suggest that rape and forced sex are desirable. Some studies show that men who rape women are more likely to have hostile attitudes toward women. The same is true for men who have nonconsensual sex with women. Researchers have found a strong correlation between negative attitudes and disrespect toward women and the proclivity for sexual assault (Lisak & Miller 2002; Edwards et al. 2014). One study concludes, in terms of attitudes toward women, college men who say they would rape a woman if they could get away with it, and those who say they would force a woman to have intercourse but don't call it rape, were distinguished only by levels of hostility and disrespect: "The two types of offender groups were distinguishable mostly by varying levels of hostility, suggesting that men who endorse using force to obtain intercourse on survey items but deny rape on the same may not experience hostile affect in response to women, but might have dispositions more in line with benevolent sexism" (Edwards et al. 2014:188). Whether college men who force nonconsensual sex buy into the pornutopic fantasy that women enjoy sexual assault whether they are conscious or unconscious, or they enjoy abusing women, it is clear that these college boys valorize nonconsensual sex.

Recent cases of creepshots found on fraternity websites, for example at Penn State, seem to confirm the conclusion that men who prey on women sexually also enjoying debasing them. For along with photographs of women in extremely compromising sexual positions, these websites include derogatory comments about the women by fraternity members. Or consider media reports of videos taken by perpetrators in the high-profile Vanderbilt rape case, which suggest that the college athletes who sexually assaulted an unconscious woman in a dorm room made derogatory remarks and jokes while engaging in the abuse. The same is true of the Steubenville (Ohio) case where high school football players assaulted an unconscious girl while bystanders joked and made disparaging remarks about her. In this case, and others, perpetrators and/or bystanders have reportedly also peed on the unconscious victims, which suggests further denigration of these girls' and women's bodies.

On many college campuses, what until recently had been called "acquaintance rape" or "date rape" has been further downgraded to "nonconsensual sex," in large part to sustain disciplinary measures that do not involve accusing the perpetrator of a felony crime, namely, rape. Campus administrators don't want to accuse their otherwise successful fraternity members (many of whose fathers were fraternity members themselves and contribute generously), or college athletes, of rape, so many are using the designation *nonconsensual sex* to refer to sexual assault, especially when the victims are unconscious.[3] The question for some administrators and members of the community seems to be, how could a leader on campus with good grades and a bright future be a rapist? Indeed, in many cases women report a backlash against them for coming forward to report sexual assault. These women often face hostility from people defending the perpetrators. This is especially true when college athletes are involved. Some colleges, for example Notre Dame, even have policies that prohibit campus police from directly approaching college athletes without contacting their coaches or athletic directors first (*The Hunting Ground* 2015). Some have argued that the move from accusations of rape to "date rape," and now to "nonconsensual sex," have been motivated by desires to protect white middle-class men, and that black men are far more likely to face accusations of rape (as opposed to nonconsensual sex or lesser charges).[4] In addition, downgrading rape to a lesser noncriminal offense excuses rape and seemingly condones rape culture.

This new category of sexual violation allows colleges and universities to discipline perpetrators who otherwise might not be found guilty of rape. On the other hand, it also turns rape into a form of sex and reduces a felony crime into a mere honor code violation. While making rape an honor code violation suggests old-fashioned ideals of chivalry that prevent men from "taking advantage" of women, it seems that attitudes toward women are at the core of sexual assault. While we may not want to return to ideals of chivalry that include putting helpless passive women on a pedestal, or rescuing princesses or damsels in distress, we do need to change attitudes of hostility and "benevolent sexism" that contribute to rape or "nonconsensual sex." As an honor code violation, students can be expelled from school for committing nonconsensual sex, but they will not be convicted or punished for the felony crime of rape.

In addition to honor codes, it is becoming more common to use Title IX of the federal civil rights law to address sexual assault on campus. Victims of sexual assault can file a Title IX complaint with the Title IX coordinator on campus (this position is required by federal law for any school receiving federal funds). Any school receiving federal funds is required to comply with Title IX, which prohibits discrimination in education based on sex. In 2011 the Department of Education sent out a "Dear Colleague Letter" to all high schools, colleges, and universities making clear that sexual harassment and sexual violence count as sex discrimination in that they interfere with educational opportunities for their victims. Unlike criminal law, which requires the higher standard of evidence "beyond a reasonable doubt," civil rights law requires the "preponderance of evidence" standard, which means that if it is more likely than not that the violation occurred, then the perpetrator should be held responsible and face consequences. In the case of colleges and universities, however, usually the harshest penalty is still expulsion, which means that serial rapists can just matriculate elsewhere and continue assaulting unsuspecting women. Unlike criminal law that requires that sex offenders be identified as such and registered, Title IX has no such requirement. Even with growing attention to sexual assault on campus, and the use of Title IX, very few students have been expelled even in cases where there is a "preponderance of evidence" that they committed sexual assault or "nonconsensual sex" (Kingkade 2014a). The federal government has never withheld funding to even a single school for noncompliance of Title IX based on sexual harassment, sexual assault, or "nonconsensual sex."

The phrase "committing nonconsensual sex" sounds odd and points to a contradiction at the heart of this notion. *Nonconsensual sex* applies to single perpetrators (as opposed to gang rape) who do not force themselves on their victims because they have already incapacitated them with drugs and/or alcohol. While, traditionally, *rape* has been defined in terms of force *and* consent, *nonconsensual sex* is defined in terms of only one of those criteria, namely consent.[5] Some conservative lawmakers have tried to distinguish between *forcible rape*, which they consider "real" rape, and what they call "mere" rape, which does not involve force, suggesting that without force, rape isn't real (Seltzer & Kelly 2012). Some feminists, on the other hand, have argued that the traditional two-pronged definition works to disqualify *both* violent consensual sex and nonconsensual sex that does not involve force (West 1996:233). The category *nonconsensual sex* may allow disciplinary action on the part of colleges and universities for sex without consent that is not forced, but it does so by again excluding nonconsensual sex from being considered rape. Of course, survivors of sexual assault can also pursue criminal charges whatever colleges and universities do or do not do to address perpetrators.

Nonconsensual sex turns on the issue of consent, specifically whether or not the alleged victim consented. In an important sense, however, consent is a state of mind, a mental state, that can be communicated or withheld, and that can change from one minute to the next.[6] In the philosophical literature, consent is typically seen as either a mental state, or a behavior or performance, or both a mental state and a behavior.[7] If consent is seen as merely a mental state, and if it is not communicated, and since others cannot necessarily intuit it, it must be solicited. This is to say, confirmation of the mental state of consent would have to be obtained through verbal communication. Given that sexual activity is itself a behavior, it may not be enough to obtain consent through the interpretation of seemingly consenting behaviors. If consent is a behavior or performance and not merely a mental state, on the other hand, the problem doesn't disappear. If consent is a behavior, then someone could give consent unintentionally by sending the wrong signals, or what one person does when to indicate consent could be different from what another person does, or consent behavior could be misinterpreted. For example, some men think that if women wear short skirts, then they're "asking for it." If consent is a matter of both mental state and behavior, then it is a feeling or state of mind that must be communicated through language or gestures. The subject must be competent to give consent, and know, at least in some sense, what she (or he) is consenting to. And therein lies the rub. Not only is it unclear what counts as a consenting behavior, but also, in terms of sexual activity, consenting to one act does not necessarily imply consent to other activities. In addition, it is unclear how to assess competence, especially in cases where both parties are intoxicated, which is often the case on college campuses. Finally, it is unclear what and how much the subject needs to know in order to consent. In other words, does sex have to become some kind of written contract to meet strict standards of consent?

Furthermore, if we think of sex as inherently a consensual activity, then "nonconsensual sex" becomes an oxymoron. *Having sex* usually refers to an activity between consenting conscious partners.[8] When one party is unconscious, common sense dictates that her consent cannot be given or assumed. Additionally, we talk about *committing crimes* like rape, but not about "committing" sex. Nonconsensual sex seemingly downgrades sexual assault and rape from a criminal offense to a breach of contract. Even former sex worker Greta Christina, whose article on what counts as sex has been widely circulated, argues that anything can count as sex so long as there is consent (1997). Consent, she claims, is the *only* necessary element that determines whether or not an activity counts as sex. As we learned from Sigmund Freud, human beings can be aroused by almost anything. But what distinguishes sex from crime is consent.

The category *nonconsensual sex* seems to be a response to the growing number of rapes that take place while the victim is unconscious or semiconscious. While it seems obvious that an unconscious person cannot give affirmative consent, this scenario, and reactions to it, throw into stark relief attitudes toward women's roles in heterosexual sex, and what it means for a woman to consent.[9] It has been the case that in order for a woman to legitimately accuse someone of rape, she was expected to actively give negative consent in the form of words or gestures. Unless a woman actively resists or says "no," her passivity or lack of protest has been interpreted as consent. In other words, doing nothing implies consent.[10] As in the myth of Sleeping Beauty, passivity implies receptivity.

More recently, policies are shifting to require affirmative consent rather than insist on negative consent. This is especially important in cases of party rape where unconscious or incapacitated girls and women are incapable of giving either negative or affirmative consent. Affirmative consent policies require verbal or nonverbal affirmative consent, which is more than merely allowing someone to do something. According to the California law, "Affirmative consent means affirmative, conscious, and voluntary agreement to engage in sexual activity" (Goldberg 2014). The law clearly states, "Lack of protest or resistance does not mean consent, nor does silence mean consent." In other words, negative consent or resistance is no longer required to prove rape.

While affirmative consent is a stronger standard than mere negative consent in that it requires that both parties actively consent either verbally or through gestures, affirmative consent should not be conflated with desire. Just because a woman submits to sex does not mean that she wants it, especially in a culture where women feel pressured to please men. As Lise Gotell argues, "even when framed through an 'only yes means yes' standard, consent is not a measure of whether a woman desires sex but, instead, whether she accedes. Consent thus functions as a sign of subordination (that is, subordination to another's power) and a means of its legitimation" (2012:372). In this regard, affirmative consent reinforces the stereotypical notion of active masculine agency and reactive feminine agency wherein the woman's power to choose is circumscribed within the very limited confines of consenting to let someone do something to her. Even affirmative consent cannot guarantee that a woman wants to have sex or a particular type of sexual activity. It only demonstrates that she acquiesces, and even positive signs of submission or affirmative consent are problematic when drugs or alcohol are involved, as they are in party rape. My analysis of new consent apps for cellphones will highlight how affirmative consent continues to legitimate men's power to set the terms of sex by recording women's consent in order to protect men from possible charges of sexual assault.

Even affirmative consent continues the tradition of treating men as the active parties to sex and women as passive or reactive. As Louise du Toit explains, "In a symbolic universe where women are seen as inherently or naturally sexually passive, or as sex objects rather than sexual subjects, a meaningful distinction between rape and normal heterosexual intercourse can only turn on the notion of a woman's consent to 'having something done to her.' . . . Normal heterosexual sex is thus where a woman consents to 'have something sexual done to her' and rape is where she doesn't consent, but it is done nevertheless. The blurred distinction between rape and normal heterosexuality is caused by the stabilization and naturalization of the polar and hierarchal opposition between active male sexuality and passive female sexuality" (du Toit 2009:50–51). While affirmative consent laws, on the other hand, make clear that heterosexual sex is still defined in terms of women submitting to the actions of others rather than women actively desiring sex themselves, considering "sex" with an unconscious girl *nonconsensual sex* rather than *rape* makes clear that within our cultural and legal norms, negative consent, that is to say, resistance, is still considered a prerequisite for counting it as rape.

Within the popular imaginary, it seems that an unconscious person does nothing to resist; she does not actively say "no." Yet she cannot *not* consent to sex any more than she can consent to it. Is the thinking of these otherwise successful fraternity brothers and college athletes who "commit nonconsensual sex" that if a girl is unconscious, then what they are doing is not rape?[11] This seems to be the case judging by the study wherein nearly a third of college men said they would force sex but wouldn't consider that rape. Of course, if the girl is unconscious, then force is not an issue. And without force, and without negative consent, these college men apparently feel entitled to use women's bodies as they please. In a culture that encourages men to feel entitled to women's bodies, where masculinity is tied to dominating women, where sex is about pleasing men, and women's passivity is interpreted as consent, unconscious women have become the serial rapists' best and easiest prey.[12]

Perhaps what is needed is an enthusiastic endorsement of desire to ensure that both parties actively and enthusiastically want to do something and both express that desire either verbally or nonverbally. In the conclusion, I propose that we consider consent in terms of its roots in feeling as a way of emphasizing the intersubjectivity of sex with partners and also the necessity for responsibility to the other's response. Returning to response ethics, in the end I argue for a notion of consent as opening up the other's response in the context of intimate communication, even in cases where sex is just for pleasure within hookup culture. As we learn from psychoanalysis, desire is complicated and always ambiguous and ambivalent. As the legend of Sleeping Beauty shows, consent can become a male projection onto his victim, whom he imagines as a properly active sexual partner, whereby he hallucinates consent, even pleasure. Sleeping Beauty may be a fairytale, but fairytales tell us something important about our cultural imaginary. As we've seen, the fourteenth-century tale of the rape of Sleeping Beauty, construed as mutually consenting sexual pleasure, is all too relevant to contemporary scenes of party rape of unconscious girls and women. When half of college men admit to aggressively pursuing sex on a date and nearly one-third of college men admit they would force a woman to have sex against her will, even if they wouldn't call it rape, it is obvious that consent is problematic. Sexual predators, including those involved in fraternity rape conspiracies previously discussed, obviously value lack of consent. They aim for nonconsensual sex, particularly through the use of drugs and alcohol to incapacitate their prey. For some of them, raping unconscious women is the ultimate power trip, completely controlling a woman's body. Even in cases where men do not intend nonconsensual sex, it is possible for men to misinterpret the gestures or signals of a woman's consent. Even if they aren't kissing her a thousand times, imagining that her unconscious lips are moving in response, "research shows that men routinely interpret women's behavior in more sexual terms than women mean or intend" (Whisnant 2013). Perceptions of consent, then, are gendered. These perceptions must be taken into account when considering issues of consent.

Education can be an important tool in addressing differing perceptions of consent, at least in the abstract. The hope is that education can provide a counterbalance, if not an antidote to pornutopic fantasies perpetuated by pornography and within popular culture. As feminists have pointed out for decades, however, much of our canonical art and literature is also based on the denigration of women and the objectification of women's bodies. If young men truly believe that unconscious girls enjoy sex, if they buy into the Sleeping Beauty fairytale or its contemporary versions in the pornutopia, then we have an uphill battle when it comes to reeducation. When highly educated boys and men at Yale University can chant, "My name is Jack, I'm a necrophiliac. I fuck dead girls," and do so in public, we have to wonder if feminists have made much progress in addressing sexism. If in the past young men harbored such fantasies, they usually hid them. Now, claiming to sexually assault and rape, and imagining unconscious girls as "dead girls," are not only acceptable behaviors among young men but also perhaps prerequisites to establish certain types of macho masculinity. Still, the hope is that education can help change our notions of masculinity and femininity such that they don't require, and perhaps don't include, violent men and women who submit to that violence.

AFFIRMATIVE CONSENT APPS FOR CELLPHONES

The prevalence of sexual assault on college campuses, and the role of alcohol, has led to affirmative consent policies at some colleges and universities. Law professor Amy Adler sees the "legal contact that is signed in *Fifty Shades of Grey*—it's kind of [the model of] what a lot of affirmative consent people are looking for. . . . Maybe we should have written, contracted-for sexual exchanges on campus in order to avoid the messiness and possibility of error that could result in rape" (Green 2015). Has *Fifty Shades of Grey* become a template for consensual sex? Given that a college student at the University of Illinois at Chicago, who is accused of raping a fellow student, claims he was reenacting scenes from the movie *Fifty Shades of Grey*, the emulation of nonconsensual sex in the context of long discussions about consent should give us pause (Holley 2015). While it's true we've become obsessed with consent, it's becoming increasingly clear that lack of consent is what has become sexy, at least in the *Fifty Shades* universe. As we have seen, in *Fifty Shades*, contractual consent in writing is opposed to real hot passionate sex, which involves a powerful man spanking a virginal college student who doesn't like it. Consent is confused with submission. In fact, for all of its problems, *Fifty Shades* makes clear the distinction between consent and submission. Although she submits, Ana clearly does not consent in that she does not sign the contract.

One tech firm has created a "consent app" for cellphones that can be used by women and men to get or deny consent, and to record it to use as proof later. The app seems primarily aimed at protecting men against charges of rape. The app records the person consenting or denying consent, and then to avoid tampering it uploads the recording to the cloud where it can only be accessed later by authorities. But this consent app does nothing to address the problem of whether or not the capacity to consent can be undermined or destroyed by drugs and alcohol. In other words, it's easy to imagine someone who is intoxicated (and still conscious) consenting verbally on this phone app even though they may be so drunk they don't know what they are doing. Some rape drugs like Ketamine may make it easy for predators to get recorded consent on cellphones if their victims remain semiconscious and susceptible to suggestion due to the drugs. In addition, the cellphone recordings would not necessarily show whether or not the woman's consent was coerced in some way. On the other hand, it is possible that the videos could "backfire" and prove that the "victim" was intoxicated and therefore could not consent.

In addition to overt coercion or threats, we should not ignore the ways in which power differentials between men and women, and sexism in our culture, coerce women into sex or sexual activities they don't want, and may therefore also coerce women into verbally consenting to sexual activities they don't want.[13] For, as Vanessa Munro reminds us, "entrenched power disparities, material inequalities, relational dynamics and socio-sexual norms operate to construct and constrain not only women's ability to say 'no' to male sexual initiative, and to have that refusal accredited both by society and law, but also—and perhaps even more problematically—to say 'yes', at least in the kind of free and unfettered way that the liberal model of autonomy often seems to presume" (2008:925). The issue of consent, then, is complicated not only by the immediate circumstances and the sobriety of the participants but also by the larger social context in which women's choices, while in principle vast, in practice are limited.

Some claim that affirmative consent is unrealistic in that sexual intimacy happens without verbal consent, and the policies do not detail what gestures (eye contact, nods, moans, smiles) constitute consent (Goldberg 2014). Consent must be reconceived when thinking about sexual relations, because unlike a contract for services, sex is an ongoing negotiation (Schulhofer 2000; McGregor 2005). Sex is a continual process of negotiation and renegotiation.[14] And, therefore, consent must be continually given as the sexual activities take place.

Consent is not a moment, but a process. And cellphone apps completely distort this fact. A woman might consent to sex without consenting to particular sexual activities or consenting to sexual assault. A woman might consent to sex on a cellphone app, but that does not mean that she consents to being forcibly raped. Consent that was freely given in the beginning can be withdrawn at any time. In fact, if we take the ability to withdraw consent at any time as definitive of consent, then an unconscious person cannot consent, and even prior consent is irrelevant.[15]

As one journalist put it, "the affirmative consent law sets the bar for sex at roughly the same level we have for going to someone's house: Don't do it if you're not invited, and don't use the fact that someone invited you into his or her living room as an excuse to abscond with a stereo" (Marcotte 2014a). Although the metaphor of a woman's body as her property is problematic, if sex is now "by invitation only," I think the better metaphor would be, don't think you can go into someone's bedroom just because they invited you into their living room; and even if they invite you into their bedroom, that doesn't mean you can do what you like there or that they can't ask you to leave at any time.

While there are advantages to requiring affirmative consent over mere negative consent in the form of resistance, we must be skeptical of affirmative consent policies that turn sex into a contract and consent into a single discrete moment, let alone affirmative consent apps for electronic devices that record the supposed moment of consent so it can to be used as evidence later. Affirmative consent continues to perpetuate stereotypical gender relations in which the man acts and the woman reacts. He has sex, while she consents to it. Taking this argument further, Lise Gotell maintains that affirmative consent normalizes certain types of masculine and feminine subjects: "The legal discourse on affirmative consent produces good masculine subjects, defined through the imperatives of seeking consent and disciplined through the risk of criminalization. Good feminine sexual subjects are, by contrast, re-action heroes, who practice agency through avoidance and who carefully anticipate the risks of sexual violence floating everywhere" (Gotell 2012:366). She concludes that it turns women into "victims in waiting" who are expected to actively fight off attacks (Gotell 2008:880). Again, women are blamed if they don't avoid risky situations that could lead to sexual assault, and if they don't aggressively fight off attacks.

In addition, gendered power relations disappear in the rhetoric of affirmative consent and choice. Affirmative consent substitutes a thin notion of sexual autonomy for sexual equity or sexual empowerment (Gotell 2012:367). The choice to consent to certain activities, or not, does not necessarily make sexual partners equal partners. The choice to consent or not does not necessarily mean that women are empowered to speak or seek to fulfill their own sexual desires, whatever they may be. Even in terms of sexual autonomy, affirmative consent is limited to the choice to acquiesce or not, which is not a very robust notion of sexual autonomy. Furthermore, insofar as affirmative consent assumes men as the active subjects of sex and women as the reactive objects, it risks repeating the very power dynamics that make rape possible in the first place.[16] Also, affirmative consent removes women from the context in which they consent. It does not, and cannot, consider why or how they consent, and whether their consent is "freely" given or coerced, whether by their sexual partner or by the sexual norms of our culture. In the words of Lise Gotell, "Affirmative consent individualizes by focusing attention on the moment of a sexual transaction, thus abstracting sexual interactions from their contexts" (Gotell 2012:361).

With affirmative consent policies, the woman's testimony to her experience of consent seems to take priority. Yet, as we have seen and will continue to see, women's testimony is often discounted in rape cases. Paradoxically, then, while in principle affirmative consent values a woman's experience of her own consent and legitimates her own testimony as to whether or not she gave consent, in practice her testimony is not taken seriously, or as seriously as a man's. Given our discussion of intoxicated consent and party rape, it is noteworthy that drunken perpetrators of rape are held *less* responsible because of intoxication while drunken victims of rape are held *more* responsible (Finch & Munro 2007:591). Intoxicated men are held less responsible while intoxicated women are blamed. Drunkenness lets men off the hook, while implicating women.

Affirmative consent apps highlight the problems with affirmative consent, most notably the notion that consent is given once, that it is a switch, either on or off, and once it is on, it stays on. These apps are obviously designed to protect men who could be accused of rape; and they are open to misuse, especially in cases where the woman consents in the beginning but changes her mind, or she consents to some activities, but not to others. Indeed, affirmative consent apps do not allow for the possibility of withdrawing consent, which is fundamental to the very concept of affirmative consent. Furthermore, insofar as these apps assume that consent is one discrete and definitive moment, they not only don't allow for withdrawing consent but also cannot adapt to changing circumstances or guarantee continued affirmative consent. Consent apps freeze consent into a moment in time that can be recorded. Even if a woman lists those activities to which she consents in a *Fifty Shades*–style contract, the most important aspect of consent is erased from these recordings, namely, the ability to withdraw consent. The ability to revoke consent is the minimal condition for the possibility of consent. Cellphone apps miss this entirely.

Still, affirmative consent in the form of "only yes means yes" seems like a step forward from assuming that silence equals consent, or worse, "no means yes." Some have argued that affirmative consent could lead to situations where women consent to sex while drunk, but regret it while sober, and later charge their sex partner with rape.[17] In the case of sexual assault on college campuses, it is important to note, if they are reported at all (and most rapes are not), they are reported to college administrators, and perpetrators never face criminal charges (Rubenfeld 2014). Also, given the low rate of reporting for rape (11.5 percent and only 2.7 percent when drugs or alcohol are involved), and given that false reporting of rape is negligible (2–6 percent), it is highly unlikely that affirmative consent policies will cause women to start "crying rape" after regretting sex the next day.[18] In fact, it is more likely that women will recant *true* accusations of sexual assault because they fear retaliation than that women will make false accusations. In other words, there is pressure on women not to report, or to recant accusations truthfully made, but there is no evidence that women regularly falsely report sexual assault.[19] Although detractors can describe situations where consent is unclear, what is clear is that women are unlikely to report consensual sex as rape.

While it is important to consider the ways in which affirmative consent policies may continue to blur the lines between consent and desire, *if enforced*, in practice they might force serial rapists to reconsider using drugs and alcohol to incapacitate their victims. Although affirmative consent does not guarantee that women want or desire sex, but rather only that they consent and submit to it, and in this regard it does not empower women to say "no" in coercive situations, the hope is that sexual predators will no longer be able to use the lack of negative consent or lack of resistance as an alibi. Of course, unless there are witnesses, or a cellphone recording, many of these cases will remain "he said, she said." What counts as evidence of consent is still an open question, especially when drugs and alcohol are involved. As we have seen, perceptions of consent vary, and studies show men are more likely to interpret certain behaviors as signs of consent than women do (Jozkowski & Peterson 2014).

If rape is defined as sex against someone's will, what if that will is compromised by drugs or alcohol to the point where the victim cannot express it? The more difficult question is when a woman doesn't *know* her own will. Perhaps the more important question is *why* she doesn't know her own will. Given pressures on young women to conform to social norms, and given that ours is still very much a patriarchal society, there are many factors that could cloud someone's judgment. This is a central problem with treating the issue of consent as one of sexual autonomy in a culture where women and others are not always fully autonomous. The stakes of determining what should count as autonomy are as high as those for what should count as consent. Indeed, without accounting for the ways in which a woman's autonomy may be compromised by her social situation, it is impossible to decipher the meaning of affirmative consent. While certainly "no" does not mean "yes," the troubling truth of patriarchy is that sometimes even "yes" does not mean "yes." *Fifty Shades of Grey* is a case in point. So too is Bogle's study of hookup culture wherein girls and women are often pressured to go farther than they want in sexual relations.

When college-age people are drinking, most of them inexperienced with sex, and some of them still teenagers, consent is a messy business. Indeed, sex often brings with it complicated emotions and cultural valuations that can make consent vexed in the best of circumstances. Men and women may feel pressured into having sex or not having sex.[20] They may feel that their masculinity or femininity is at stake. They may want different things from the experience before and after, or even during. There can be misunderstandings and miscommunication. Recall studies that indicate that women are pressured to go farther than they want, and that perceptions of consent are gendered (Bogle 2008; Burnett et al. 2009; Jozkowski & Peterson 2014). And now that attention is given to the role of college drinking in sexual assault, and the incapacitation of judgment on the part of both perpetrators and victims when intoxicated, the standard of rape has shifted from the question of force to the question of consent. Certainly, many cases of rape on college campuses involve force, whether or not they are acquaintance or date rapes. But with so many high-profile cases involving severely intoxicated college students, and in some cases victims who are unconscious, the question of physical force becomes moot.

The lack of force in these cases is another reason why the designations "rape" or "sexual assault," both of which traditionally refer to the use of force, no longer seem to apply in a straightforward way. If the victim is already incapacitated due to drugs or alcohol, then physical force may be unnecessary on the part of the perpetrator, particularly if the victim is unconscious. In these cases, nonconsensual sex does not require force. The victims of these crimes may arrive at the hospital or rape crisis center without any visible signs of assault. As we move from designations of *rape*, through *sexual assault*, to *nonconsensual sex*, we move from situations of sexual assault involving battery, to ones in which the victim may not have been physically damaged, and where physical force may not have been necessary to subdue the victim.[21]

Obviously, given the problem of sexual assault and rape on college campuses, especially those involving drugs and alcohol, the issue of consent takes center stage. The difference between rape and sex is consent. Consent works its *moral magic* and transforms an act from impermissible to permissible (Hurd 1996). If the accused can convince a university board or a jury that the woman consented, then he is exonerated. For example, Heisman trophy winner Jamies Winston's DNA was in a rape kit while he celebrated his success. Like many cases of sexual assault or rape, it became a "he said, she said' situation, in which it was his word against his accuser, who was harassed by Florida State University football fans after she came forward with rape allegations. Without evidence of force, evidence of rape drugs, or witnesses, it becomes difficult to prove consent or lack of it.

It is assumed that an unconscious person cannot give affirmative consent. But there is still the question of whether or not an unconscious person can give negative consent, which has been de facto required to prove that rape took place. Furthermore, some have raised the question of whether or not advance consent can be given for activities that take place while unconscious—for example, the initiation of sex with a sleeping partner, the so-called problem of the sleeping spouse.[22] While reasonable people may conclude that an unconscious person cannot give consent of any kind, and therefore sex with an unconscious person is always nonconsensual sex, consciousness is not always simply an off-or-on proposition, especially when drugs or alcohol are involved. In some of the most high-profile cases recently, the victims have been completely unconscious at the time of the sexual assaults, evidenced by photographs showing their limp bodies being dragged and tossed like rag dolls. But in other cases involving alcohol, even cases where the victim does not remember being raped and learns about it later through creepshots taken by the perpetrator or bystanders, there are questions of what counts as consent and how much consciousness or incapacitation is necessary to declare someone able to consent or unable to consent. Where do we draw the line in terms of intoxicated consent? In other words, if consciousness is a prerequisite for consent, at what point is consciousness impaired enough to prohibit the possibility of consent? This question is especially relevant when we consider the role of drinking in rape, date rape, sexual assault, and nonconsensual sex. At what point does a woman become incompetent to give consent?[23] In the case of drunken college students, is there a blood alcohol level at which they no longer are able to give consent? And should the same standards apply to men as to women? In other words, if two severely intoxicated students have sex, are they raping each other?

David Archard argues that, given the significant harm to women if they are forced to have sex against their will, or when they do not consent to sex, and given the relative lack of harm to men if they abstain from sex, it is the man's responsibility to obtain affirmative consent from the woman (1998:144–45). Furthermore, Archard argues that men know when they are having sex, and usually they are also aware of their partner's reactions, especially signs of nonconsent. He concludes, "men have a duty to take reasonable care lest women do not consent. The costs of taking such care are not great and are certainly insignificant when compared to the costs that are avoided by such care being taken" (1998:145). In Archard's view, which is reasonable if not completely satisfactory, it is a man's responsibility to avoid nonconsensual sex. And it is a man's responsibility to obtain affirmative consent. Until we change rape culture and attitudes toward women, unfortunately, this may be the best stopgap solution; namely, to hold men responsible for consent. As discussed earlier, however, this type of policy is problematic insofar as it gives men the primary responsibility. Of course, it is appropriate that the primary responsibility *not* to sexually assault women (or other men) lies with those who are in a position to do so. Men should be required to get active consent from their partners. In spite of its conceptual problems, holding men primarily responsible for getting consent is pragmatically necessary, especially in a culture that increasingly fetishizes the moment of consent, the association between consent and contracts, and too often leaves us with "he said, she said" legal proceedings that are not adequate to address sexual assault.

Where alcohol rather than force is used to incapacitate, what counts as consent and what counts as rape becomes even more problematic.[24] Although it is crucial to note that the use of drugs and alcohol does not cause sexual assault, they are an important component of rape on college campuses. As one study of the correlation between alcohol use and rape puts it, "even though many sexual assaults involve substance use by the victim, this does not imply that women are in any way responsible for their sexual assault. Victimization is committed by the perpetrator, and prevention programs targeting university men should strongly emphasize that an intoxicated or incapacitated person cannot legally or otherwise consent to sexual contact" (Krebs et al. 2009:643). Of course, when drugs and alcohol are involved and the judgment of both parties is impaired, this may be easier said than done, which is not to say that men should not be held responsible for having sex with incapacitated women. But the issue of consent gets messy when drunken men and women are trying to interpret signs of consent, or behaving in ways that could be interpreted as consent.

Take, for example, a case in 2013 at Occidental College, where "John Doe" was expelled from college for sexual misconduct after having sex with "Jane Doe" when she was intoxicated. They both were drunk. She had been taken back to her own dorm room by friends but subsequently returned to John Doe's dorm room to "have sex" as she texted a friend that night. She was a virgin at the time. Later, although she didn't deny going to his room, she claimed that she was too drunk to consent to sex. This is probably a typical situation on college campuses. Both parties are drunk. They have sex. One or both regret it the next day. Whose responsibility is it to obtain consent? Whose consent matters? Whose consent makes the difference between rape or nonconsensual sex and just poor judgment? In cases such as the one at Occidental where signs of consent were apparently given, but by a severely intoxicated woman, it may be appropriate for colleges and universities to discipline students using their honor codes rather than criminal or even civil law. Should just the male student be disciplined in such a case (of male-on-female sexual assault)? In an age of sexual freedom and autonomy, this may sound too "old-fashioned." Yet if colleges and universities are downgrading rape to "nonconsensual sex," and if the punishment is expulsion rather than years in prison, then perhaps the tradeoff is that affirmative consent policies can help stop rape on campus.[25] Furthermore, it seems appropriate to consider underage drinking and sex with incapacitated or severely intoxicated women an honor code violation. Off campus, underage drinking and nonconsensual sex are still crimes. Why is it any different on campus? The answer, of course, is that colleges and universities attract undergraduates by allowing the party atmosphere that appeals to students and makes college fun. If, for example, a college or university prohibited drinking on campus, that would definitely cut down on the numbers of applications it received. Some schools have a reputation as "party schools" and some students seek out these institutions.

Sexual assaults involving alcohol in the military have led to the "Ask Her When She's Sober" poster campaign.[26] Only recently has there been much attention given to rape in the military, even though according to the Pentagon's own Rand Report, approximately one-third of the women soldiers in Iraq and Afghanistan have been raped or sexually assaulted by their fellow soldiers.[27] In 2013, Lieutenant Colonel Jeffrey Krusinski, who was in charge of sexual assault prevention programs for the Air Force, was himself charged with sexual battery, and two weeks later a sexual abuse educator at Fort Hood (Texas) was charged with sexual assault and running a prostitution ring, and, at the same time, reports of military recruiters across the country engaging in sex crimes hit the press. This chain of sex crimes was coincident with a new Pentagon study on the pervasive sexual abuse in the military, which reports that there was an average of three sexual assaults an hour in 2012, and many more that go unreported (Brook and Zoroya 2013). Suddenly, the Pentagon was in the middle of what the *Washington Post* called a "sex-crime crisis" (Whitlock 2012).

The military's response to its sex-crime crisis has also come under scrutiny—especially with reports that one military chaplain advised an army sergeant who was raped by a fellow soldier that "the rape must have been God's will and that she should go to church more often" (Mulrine 2012), and that an Air Force brochure on sexual assault tells victims to submit rather than resist, which runs counter to research that shows that fighting back can fend off the attacker and usually does not lead to greater injury (Ackerman 2013). The brochure also says that rapists look for those who are vulnerable, namely the young, naïve, or emotionally unstable (Ackerman 2013). All of this, combined with other military responses such as the Army's poster advising servicemen to "Ask Her When She's Sober," suggests the classic blame-the-victim approach to rape in the military.

Moreover, military culture discourages reporting rapes. From the boot-camp mentality, to the fact that reporting sexual assault ruins military careers, to the fact that very few military rapists are convicted and sentenced to prison, many victims of rape in the military do not report it (Whitlock 2012; Lawrence & Peñaloza 2013).

Myla Haider, a former agent in the Army's Criminal Investigation Command and a rape victim herself, says, "I've never met one victim who was able to report the crime and still retain their military career. Not one" (Lawrence & Peñaloza 2013). Haider herself was kicked out of the Army after reporting her rape. Although college women aren't expelled from school for reporting rape, many of them are run off campus by harassment, especially when they accuse popular athletes.[28]

RETALIATION FOR REPORTING AND PERPETRATORS CLAIMING VICTIMHOOD

Accusing top athletes and white middle-class honors students of rape is difficult. Often the community rallies around the alleged perpetrator and discounts the testimony of the alleged victim, who may suffer harassment or retaliation for accusing a star athlete. This was the case of Heisman trophy winner and alleged rapist Jamies Winston at Florida State University and his accuser Erica Kinsman. While he won awards, she was forced to leave FSU. ESPN commentators Skip Bayless and Stephen A. Smith described the allegations against Winston as "terribly unfair" and suspiciously timed (even though Kinsman had reported the alleged rape a year before) (Glock 2015).[29] The community came to his defense and harassed her. He was celebrated while she was castigated. At this writing, he is suing her for defamation of character, even though his DNA was found in the rape kit and another woman had also accused him of sexual misconduct. Kinsman claims that Winston and his friends put something in her drink and that is how she ended up in Winston's apartment. Winston claims the sex was consensual.

Women report being harassed for reporting rape, or for standing up against rape on campus. This harassment adds another layer of trauma to the sexual assault (Ullman & Peter-Hagene

2014). The public too often sides with the perpetrators, especially when they are star athletes or popular fraternity brothers. Rape victims are routinely asked about what they were wearing, what they did to provoke the attack, whether or not they resisted, and if their actions might have been construed as consent, and so on. The documentary *The Hunting Ground* shows dozens of young women who suffered additional trauma after reporting their rapes, when college administrators and police didn't seem to believe them. One survivor, Annie Clark, recounts an administrator told her, "rape is like a football game," and asked her if she were the quarterback what she might have done differently. This kind of blame-the-victim mentality is commonplace, especially on college campuses where young women dress up and drink at fraternity parties.[30] Women are further traumatized when authorities don't take them seriously, blame them, or side with their attackers. Not being taken seriously contributes to PTSD symptoms by making women question themselves, and women suffer more shame along with feelings of helplessness.[31] In addition, they may have to watch while their attackers not only go free but are heralded as the true victims, while they are painted as the evil ones, ruining promising college men's careers.

Survivors who come forward are subjected to smear campaigns, backlash on social media sites, and in some cases even lawsuits by the accused. Men accused of rape "fight back" by discrediting their accusers. They take up the position of the victim, arguing that they have been damaged by accusations, or that their futures have been ruined. Turning the tables, they attempt to make the sexual assault survivor into a libelous attacker and make themselves into the innocent victim. For example, in the now high-profile case of Emma Sulkowicz, also known as "mattress girl," her fellow Columbia University student who allegedly anally raped her, in what started as consensual sex and progressed into violent forced anal penetration against her protests, is now suing Columbia University and Sulkowicz's senior thesis advisor, who allowed her to carry a mattress as part of her senior performance project.

FIGURE 2.1 Emma Sulkowicz's performance art "Carry That Weight."

The alleged rapist accuses the alleged victim of harassment. He claims that her performance was "bullying" him. The mattress performance, called "Carry That Weight," was designed to raise awareness of rape on campus. Sulkowicz vowed to carry the mattress on which she was raped until her rapist was brought to justice. Now, the accused claims that he is the real victim in the case. When Sulkowicz carried her mattress to a graduation ceremony, posters appeared around campus calling her a "pretty little liar"; and while she has received praise for her courage and for her performance art, she has also received threats.

Sulkowicz's case may be unique because the university endorsed her performance project, and more importantly it was subsequently taken up in positive ways by mainstream media. In general, however, because of differing access to media, and public acceptance of rape myths that see the survivors as sluts, women continue to be muted about their experiences of sexual assault. In fact, studies have shown that "women have been muted in a multitude of ways, including methods in which women tell stories, through male-controlled media, in ways women's bodies are portrayed and analyzed, and through censorship of women's voices (Houston & Karamarae 1994). Men, on the other hand, not only feel more comfortable and confident in using the dominant communicative system, they also trust institutions more than women do, since institutions are created and named by men" (Burnett et al. 2009). Notably, several websites hosted by men's groups advise men on what to do if they are accused of rape. Some of these sites suggest that feminists may falsely accuse men just to target them and harass them. Some of these sites portray the accused as the true victim of feminists. Many of these sites give advice on how men can protect themselves from prosecution if accused.[32]

In the highly visible cases in Steubenville (Ohio) where high school football players sexually assaulted an unconscious girl, and in Nashville (Tennessee), where Vanderbilt University football players sexually assaulted a college junior, much of the initial public response was talk of promising football careers ruined. In cases involving popular athletes, there is often more concern for how the rape affects the perpetrator than how it affects the victim. This silencing contributes to, and perpetuates, rape culture on college campuses. Survivors are discouraged from coming forward, especially if the perpetrator is an athlete or a well-respected fraternity brother. And when they do come forward, as in the case of Erica Kinsman, they may suffer public harassment.

In the documentary *The Hunting Ground* (2015), many women who reported rapes, and the two women at the center of anti-rape activism, Annie Clark and Andrea Pino, describe how they continue to be harassed and even receive death threats.[33] Pino says, "There is more of a deterrent for coming forward than actually committing rape. And it is more likely that the survivor will drop out before an assailant will leave campus. Nobody is expelled, nobody goes to prison, so it continues to be a part of college life" (Pino qtd. in Glock 2015). At the extreme, the harassment of victims can be deadly. For example, at the University of Mary Washington, Grace Rebecca Mann was harassed via social media, especially on the anonymous app Yik Yak, and eventually murdered for speaking out against fraternities that encouraged rape, and against the rugby team in particular for a song praising sexual assault and necrophilia (Dewan & Stolberg 2015). This rugby team and these fraternities, however, do not just represent isolated incidents or "a few bad apples." As we've seen, fraternities across the country are coming under fire for songs, chants, and social media sites that encourage sexual assault and rape. Some fraternities have been sanctioned for hosting parties where they serve rape drug–spiked punch to girls in order to intentionally incapacitate them in sexual assault conspiracies. The explicit goal of these parties, as suggested by chants of "No means yes" or "My name is Jack, I'm a necrophiliac, I fuck dead girls," is nonconsensual sex with unconscious girls.

"DEAD GIRLS," UNCONSCIOUS VICTIMS, AND PUBLIC SHAME

Recent cases make vivid the corpse-like nature of unconscious girls who are sexually assaulted and raped. Girls who are unconscious when raped, and then learn about their rape later through photographs, are literally forced to see their rape through the eyes of their rapists and the bystanders who saw it as a "Facebook" moment. They are forced to see their bodies as *living corpses* through the eyes of witnesses who claim they look "dead" and "lifeless."[34] Louise du Toit's discussion of the rape victim's experience of her own body as a "living corpse" takes on a new and powerful meaning in light of creepshots and video recordings of sexual assaults. Victims view their own lifeless bodies being dragged, dropped, violated, abused, and raped, not as participants in the scene, but as observers of it. Further alienating them from their own experience and their own bodies, viewing their bodies as having undergone abuses that they don't remember intensifies the damage to the victims' sense of their own identity and the coherence of their experience. It works to undermine their confidence in their own ability to know themselves.[35]

Louise du Toit claims the damage rape does to victims is to make them see their own bodies through the eyes of their rapists as passive objects, and to see their own agency through the eyes of their rapists as powerless. The victim is treated like a thing. For the rapist her body has the advantages of a "corpse"—it can be used and abused with abandon—without the disadvantages, its abjection or putrefaction.[36] The victim is forced to confront her own mortality and her body as a corpse. It splits her experience into seeing her body as a corpse while experiencing it as a living body; she becomes a sort of living corpse. Of course, du Toit is speaking metaphorically when she talks of the corpse-like feeling of victims who were conscious of their attacks. She is not talking about recent cases of unconscious girls whose limp bodies were dragged around, violated, and described as "dead girls" completely "lifeless," a living corpse. For girls and women who are victims of nonconsensual sex, sexual assault, or rape while unconscious, referred to as "dead girls" by their rapists, and later shown pictures of their own inanimate bodies being violated, the perception of their bodies as a living corpse is even more dramatic.

Discovering that one has been raped while unconscious can cause different types and levels of harm more severe than the trauma of sexual assault while awake.[37] The fact that victims discover their victimization from third parties or recordings undermines a sense of coherent existence that cuts to the heart of the sense of self. It is as if this happened to someone else and yet it undeniably did not. The victim may come to question herself, to experience her life as fragmented, and to fear unconsciousness, even sleep. As Cressida Heyes argues, "women who have been sexually assaulted while unconscious report that they become hyper-vigilant, unable to close their eyes for fear of losing control and becoming vulnerable again" (Heyes forthcoming). Rape while unconscious damages the victim's sense of herself as an agent in ways unique to this form of rape. Heyes concludes, "Sexual assault in these situations, and especially rape . . . exploits and reinforces a victim's lack of agency and exposes her body in ways that make it especially difficult for her to reconstitute herself as a subject. It damages both her ability to engage with the world in four dimensions (through a temporally persisting body schema), and her ability to retreat from it into anonymity. . . . Deviations and interruptions in the stream of sensory perception, and the anonymity unconsciousness (usually experienced as sleep) provides are just as important to subjectivity" (Heyes forthcoming). Victims who are raped while unconscious or asleep may find restful sleep impossible, fearing that if they go to sleep or pass out, they will be attacked again. Furthermore, they no longer can rely on the "anonymity of sleep," a time when every living creature requires a safe space to retreat from the world.[38] The anonymity of sleep is further disturbed if images of the victim's sleeping body are disseminated through social media. What should be a time of restful recovery and restoration becomes a dangerous time of special vulnerability to sexual assault followed by ridicule through social media. Heyes's analysis both does and does not apply to cases where girls and women are drugged or pass out from alcohol. Their unconscious state is not exactly the same as sleeping. And the use of rape drugs to render victims unconscious is far more pernicious than disturbing sleep.

Perpetrators can continue their victimization of targets of sexual assault using social media. Posting photographs and jeering comments extends the damage to victims beyond the rape itself. "Sexual assault is a crime of power and dominance," says psychologist Rebecca Campbell. "By distributing images of the rape through social media, this is a way of asserting dominance and power to hurt the victim over and over again" (qtd. in Fuchs et al. 2013). Rape has become a spectator sport in which rapists pose for the camera and victims are subject to creepshots distributed or posted as trophies or entertainment, which adds a new layer of trauma and shame onto these crimes. Social media adds insult to injury for many victims, whether or not they are seeing their rape for the first time on a computer screen. Photographs and videos have been used to further torment and shame victims, adding another layer of victimization to the sexual assault itself.[39] The trauma of victimization not only becomes public but also infinitely repeatable. It can go viral. It doesn't go away. Its presence on social media extends the victimization and trauma into an infinite future that makes closure or healing more difficult, if not impossible.[40]

Indeed, the shame over photographs of their naked bodies in compromising positions being treated as living corpses has led some victims to kill themselves rather than face public scorn. For example, in April 2013, in two distinct cases, teenage girls killed themselves after photographs of their sexual assaults were posted online (Fuchs et al. 2013). In text messages, they both suggested that they couldn't go on living with the public shame of everyone seeing their violated bodies. Many rape survivors feel shame over being sexually assaulted, even if when they don't blame themselves, and even when only their perpetrator knows about it. Social media and the public spectacle of party rape intensify this shame and add another layer of degradation, namely, the humiliation of being photographed while compromised and victimized. The dissemination of creepshot photographs of sexual assault adds another type of trauma to the trauma of sexual assault. Friends and strangers, anyone with access to the Internet, might see pictures that compound the trauma of sexual assault and take its harms to another level.[41]

According to a government report, "Victims of sexual assault are more likely to suffer academically and from depression, posttraumatic stress disorder, to abuse alcohol and drugs, and to contemplate suicide."[42] Suicide.org reports that 33 percent of rape victims contemplate suicide and 13 percent of rape victims will commit suicide (Caruso n.d.). Many feminists have discussed the devastating effects of rape on victims.[43] For example, du Toit claims that the victim's world is "unmade" (2009). Discussing her own rape, Susan Brison says, "I felt as if I was experiencing things posthumously," which resonates with the idea of one's own body as a living corpse (2003:8). Brison and du Toit discuss this living corpse–like experience for rape victims who are aware of their rapes, relive them, testify to them, and continue to be traumatized by the experience of them afterwards. But for a woman who sees her rape for the first time through the eyes of others, this experience of one's own body as not one's own, as one's own body as a living corpse, can only be intensified. And for women whose sexual assault is documented, recorded, and posted on social media, the reliving of the incident and the retraumatization is extended indefinitely.

Discussing the specific harm of rape, Ann Cahill argues, "rape, in its total denial of the victim's agency, will, and personhood, can be understood as a denial of intersubjectivity itself" (2001:132). Rendering their victims unconscious is an effective way to avoid dealing with the intersubjectivity usually involved in having sex, consensual or nonconsensual. Sexual predators deny intersubjectivity by using rape drugs and alcohol to ensure that their victims are not conscious or only semiconscious. This strategy not only makes it easier to rape girls and women but also allows the perpetrator to avoid the intersubjective dimension of sex. In these scenarios, girls and women function as living dolls with which boys and men pleasure themselves. Consider too that within the pornutopia, there is only one subject who matters. His desires are supposedly mirrored by hers. Furthermore, the widespread exposure to pornography, and use of pornography for their first sexual experiences, may lead boys and men to expect one-directional sex in which they are the actors and their sexual partners are like the two-dimensional women on their computer screens. If use of pornography is the norm for many sexual experiences, then sex without true intersubjective encounters is becoming the norm. Certainly, drugs and alcohol can leech the victim's subjectivity from the scene and make her more like an object or living corpse than a sex partner, or even a resisting victim. Drugs and alcohol may render the victim more like the two-dimensional object of pornography insofar as she doesn't respond, but the unconscious woman has the "advantage" of being a fleshy other, unlike the pornographic object. In this way, on the level of the imaginary of the rapist, the victim's unconsciousness may work to absolve him of the crime insofar as he can justify it by saying, "what she doesn't know won't hurt her." Or, as one participant claimed in the Steubenville (Ohio) rape case, "we don't know whether or not she wanted it." Like the rapist prince in the legend of Sleeping Beauty, or the masculine subject of the pornutopia, these perpetrators may even imagine that their victims enjoyed it.

The growing use of rape drugs and alcohol to render girls unconscious, and thereby easily "rapeable," combined with sentiments expressed in the Yale fraternity chant, "My name is Jack, I'm a necrophiliac, I fuck dead girls," suggest a valorization and eroticization of sex with unconscious girls. Consider, for example, in 2014, a fraternity at the University of Wisconsin planned a party to incapacitate "hot" girls using punch spiked with the drug Rohypnol; the girls were given an all-you-can-drink pass, and their hands were marked with a red-X, presumably so that fraternity brothers could easily make out their targets.[44] Several girls ended up in the hospital. Rape drugs can be lethal at high doses. It is unclear whether or not the "rape conspiracy" was successful at the University of Wisconsin. If the girls were drugged unconscious and had no memory of sexual assault, how would we know, unless the perpetrators confessed or the hospitals used rape kits? Using drugs like Rohypnol help ensure that the victim can't testify against her rapist, especially if she remains unconscious during the entire attack. What is clear is that in cases involving date rape drugs, the goal on the part of perpetrators is to incapacitate their victims and make them easy prey for sexual assault. The goal is to have sex with a passive, unconscious, unresponsive, "lifeless" girl. Lack of consent is assumed. Nonconsensual sex with an unconscious woman puts the man in complete control of the woman's body. Certainly, "sex" with inanimate girls is not about intimacy, and perhaps not even pleasure, but control. These fraternity boys are trophy-hunting for prime party rape prey. As the Yale chant suggests, these fraternity boys and men want sex with "dead girls."

Perhaps this valorization and eroticization of sex with so-called "dead girls," a form of pseudo-necrophilia, is also a product of pornography, especially zombie porn or snuff porn. If intelligent college students want to have sex with unconscious girls, this form of pseudo-necrophilia as the ultimate macho sexual power trip has become eroticized in our culture. Of course, social media is filled with pornographic images of naked women, whether it is professionally made porn, pornographic selfies, or creepshots. Pornography has penetrated mainstream culture, not just with the prevalence and availability of pornography on the Internet, but also in our everyday lives (Green 2015).[45] The "mainstream penetration" of pornography is evident in "the way people are presenting themselves for cameras," which "is much more sexualized than it once was" (Green 2015). A century ago, people looked stone-faced into cameras. A couple of decades ago, people smiled for the camera. Now, people—particularly girls and young women—pucker their lips and make a "sexy" face, familiar from porn. The Internet is full of pornographic selfies.

It is noteworthy that in most of the recent high-profile rape cases there have been groups of boys or young men involved, some of whom take photos and videos using cellphones. This also suggests that rape has become a spectator sport worthy of candid photographs to be disseminated during and after the event. These boys and young men are "having fun," and they see the photographs of naked "dead" girls in compromising positions as "funny."[46] Pseudo-necrophilia has gone mainstream. Discussing the horror film *Deadgirl* (2008), in which a living-corpse zombie girl is repeatedly raped and abused by high school boys, film critic Steve Jones says, "we are left with the horror that Deadgirl is an erotic object because she epitomizes powerlessness" (Jones 2013:532). Has absolute powerlessness on the part of girls and women become the height of a new erotic fantasy? Has this form of pseudo-necrophilia become a new norm for sex on college campuses? Recent cases of sexual assault on unconscious girls suggest that something about the victim's complete powerlessness and lack of agency has become erotic, fun, or even funny. In addition to the eroticization of unconscious women, then, it is crucial to consider the power dynamics in sexually violating someone powerless to resist. Raping an unconscious woman is the ultimate power trip, proving absolute dominance over another human being, and a woman in particular. Pictures of sexual assault have become new forms of trophies mounted on the Internet.

Some scholars have argued that sports culture, military culture, and other aspects of dominant culture, including movies and video games, promote the idea that masculinity is gained and proved by dominating girls and women, especially through sex and rape.[47] Although rape and the connection to masculinity is not new, it is particularly troubling that rape is becoming openly valorized, as evidenced by groups of college men chanting rape slogans, and the value put on lack of consent, also endorsed in these slogans. Rape is becoming a group activity with spectators. In some cases, it is even a planned event, as for example in the fraternities accused of "rape conspiracy" for serving punch spiked with rape drugs in order to incapacitate their "rapebait" (Frampton 2015; Schwaarz 2015). While there always has been rape, including gang rape, what seems new is the public valorization of "nonconsensual sex" and its display on social media. If, in the past, rapists acted in the shadows and kept their acts a secret, now they chant in public about rape, they record their sexual assaults, and they post pictures of them for entertainment online. Rape has become a form of public entertainment.

RECORDING NOT REPORTING: "PICTURES DON'T LIE" (EVEN IF WOMEN DO)

Ironically, in some recent high-profile cases, because the victims were unconscious—and in some cases didn't even know they had been raped—rape was easier to prove, try, and convict. This suggests that the "testimony" of unconscious girls is more believable than that of conscious ones. Many feminists have discussed the ways in which victim blaming and victim shaming contribute to the low number of women who report rape (2.5–11 percent), along with extremely low conviction rates for rape (as low as 5 percent), which also may contribute to low reporting (Anderson 2003:78; Caringella 2008; Wolitzky-Taylor et al. 2011; Kim 2012). In addition, many of these same scholars have discussed the ways in which the victim's testimony is discounted.[48] Furthermore, as we have seen, studies show that when authorities don't believe victims, this significantly contributes to levels and duration of trauma that result from sexual assault (Ullman & Peter-Hagene 2014).

The documentary *The Hunting Ground* shows dozens of college women discussing how they were blamed for their own rapes and how the perpetrators were never punished in any way. Many of the young women talked as if the fact that the perpetrators were not punished, and in some cases even celebrated as star athletes, was as traumatic as the rape itself. They were made to feel as if they were responsible for their own victimization, which was compounded by the perpetrators being seemingly unaffected. When perpetrators go free, sometimes even defended or celebrated, it makes victims feel out of touch with reality and undermines their feelings of legitimacy. In one heart-wrenching scene in *The Hunting Ground*, a father recounts how his daughter killed herself after it became clear that her perpetrator was going to get away with it. A rape conviction, or at least some disciplinary action taken against the perpetrator, legitimates the victim's testimony and sense of her own experience. Many young women in the documentary expressed hurt and frustration by the fact that the rape had damaged their lives forever, while their perpetrators seemingly faced no consequences for their actions. Many remarked on the "unfairness" of this situation where they are violated, blamed, and then left to face a trauma that may take years from which to recover, if ever, while their rapists go about their lives, business as usual, in many cases continuing to sexually assault other women.

While the testimony of young women is challenged, discounted, and often at best put into the context of a "he said, she said" situation, the recent phenomenon of creepshot photographs of rapes, and the recording of unconscious rape victims taken with cellphone cameras, has brought about some high-profile convictions. As one detective said in the Vanderbilt rape case, "pictures don't lie" (20/20 2015). In spite of statistics that false reporting is extremely low, too often the suspicion is that rape victims can, and do, lie.[49] Certainly the case of "Jackie," who reported a terrible gang rape at the University of Virginia, as covered by *Rolling Stone*, which subsequently turned out to be false, didn't help the cause of rape victims.[50] In some recent high-profile cases, however, the victim didn't even know she had been raped. In these cases, the rape was recorded and not reported. In these cases, it seems that the mute "testimony" of a visually "lifeless," "dead girl" is more powerful than the sorrowful testimony of victims aware of their attacks.

For example, on June 23, 2013, an unconscious Vanderbilt honor's student was gang-raped by four Vanderbilt football players, two of whom were later convicted on all counts, and two of whom have yet to stand trial, as of this writing.[51] One of the convicted rapists, Brandon Vandenburg, had been going out with the victim at the time. After a night of drinking at a local restaurant bar, he enlisted friends to help haul his girlfriend into his dorm room after she passed out in her car. He took pictures of her being sodomized with a water bottle and by his teammate Corey Batey, and sent them to friends. The victim has no memory of the rapes. The next day, Vandenburg reportedly told her that she'd vomited in his room and he'd taken care of her all night. Embarrassed, she thanked him.

Two days later, investigating vandalism in the dorm, campus police saw surveillance videos of the football players dragging the unconscious woman down the hallway of the dorm, taking her into

Vandenburg's room, then going in and out of the dorm room, and at one point covering the surveillance camera with a towel. That surveillance video, which aired on the television show 20/20, showed the men dragging the half-naked unconscious woman, dropping her several times, giggling, smiling, and happily taking pictures of her, even close-ups of her butt. Supposedly, Vandenburg's roommate was asleep on the top bunk during part of the assault and later left the room. Several other men in the dorm saw the football players manhandling the unconscious woman, several men saw the videos of the rape, even while it was going on, and not one of them reported it to authorities. Two of Vandenburg's friends in California received photos and videos throughout the night, one of them commenting in a message back to Vandenburg that they should "gang bang" the "bitch," make sure she "doesn't wake up," and then "get rid of her."

By the end of the investigation, police had confiscated cellphone photographs and videos of Corey Batey raping the unconscious girl and Brandon Banks sodomizing her with a bottle. All the while, Vandenburg was taking photos, laughing, and egging them on. Reportedly, he tried to rape her too, but couldn't "get it up" because he had done too much cocaine. In their own words, the players were "clowning" for the camera. They were taking pictures as if they were on vacation, to show their sexual prowess, and because they thought it was funny. As authorities started questioning them, the players met to plan their strategy. They deleted the videos and photographs. Vandenburg instructed his friends in California to destroy their cellphones, which they did. But one of their phones had automatically uploaded the video to his computer and eventually the police found it. At first, the victim denied that she'd been raped. She couldn't believe it. The police had to show her the photographs and videos in order to prove it to her. When interviewed, the detectives said this was the first time that they had to convince the victim that she'd been raped. Rather than being reported, the rape was recorded.

As strange as it seems, recording instead of reporting is becoming more common. Girls are finding out they've been raped when pictures taken by the rapists or bystanders are posted on social media or sent around as text messages. For example, on August 11, 2012, in Steubenville (Ohio), an unconscious high school student was sexually assaulted while bystanders watched. Photographs and videos that circulated on social media showed the perpetrators talking about rape while assaulting her. Later, texts and tweets also joked about rape, making light of the fact that the girl was "so raped," and slept through "a wang in the butthole" (Ley 2012). Two boys on the football team were found guilty in juvenile court. And several adults were charged with trying to cover up the crime or hinder the investigation. Reportedly, the football coach threatened a journalist covering the case, and the school superintendent tampered with evidence. The victim didn't know that she'd been raped until she saw the pictures. The boy who posted photographs was found guilty of distributing child pornography since the girl was underage.[52] One of the perpetrators defended himself, saying, "It isn't really rape because you don't know if she wanted to or not" (Ley 2013). This sentiment makes clear that in these young people's minds, or at least in this person's mind, consent and desire are not only mental states but also the same mental state.[53] Furthermore, the fantasy is that if a girl is unconscious, and neither affirmative nor negative consent can be given, "sex" with her is not really rape. Echoing the age-old myth of Sleeping Beauty, along with her pornutopic sisters who enjoy being raped, these boys imagined their unconscious victim actually might be consenting, perhaps even "wanting" it.

Many rape cases that come to light via social media or cellphone photographs feature groups of people, mostly men, watching as unconscious girls are dragged, dropped, sexually abused, and photographed. Some of these bystanders take pictures with their phones rather than report the crimes. In these cases, cellphones become part of the sexual assault. Rapists and bystanders take pictures for fun or entertainment, and generally to enhance the experience. They have even more fun distributing the pictures to friends or on social media sites. Take, for example, a young woman who first discovered she had been gang-raped on Panama City beach in Florida when a video appeared on the nightly news. Hundreds of people watched. Seemingly part of the scenery or entertainment on that crowded beach, someone had recorded it using a cellphone (Stapleton & Levs 2015). Reportedly, she was drugged with a drink offered to her on the beach and then two Troy University (Alabama) students sexually assaulted her. A spokesperson for the local sheriff's office said, "there's a number of videos we've recovered with things similar to this, and I can only imagine how many things we haven't recovered . . . through social media we have been able to find video of girls, incoherent and passed out, and almost like they are drugged, being assaulted on the beaches of Panama City in front of a bunch of people standing around" watching (Stapleton & Levs 2015). A popular Spring Break destination for college students, Florida beaches are also a hotspot for college rapists who prey on intoxicated girls. Perhaps as troubling as the sexual assault itself is the fact that rather than helping the victims, bystanders just watch or take videos and post them online.

Pictures of unconscious girls in compromising positions are sent around like funny cat videos. While these images retraumatize the victim, and celebrate sexual violation, they can also be used as hard evidence of sexual assault or rape, which, as we've seen, is notoriously difficult to prove, and even more difficult to prosecute and convict.[54] Pictures and videos taken as part of the "fun" of sexual assault can be used to convince a jury that assault took place (BBC Staff 2015). They also are making it apparent to our culture at large that sexual violence is considered "fun" and "funny" by lots of young people who enjoy a good party, especially if it involves unconscious girls.[55] But, as we've seen, for victims, their humiliation can go viral and seemingly last forever on social media (Grinberg 2013). As noted earlier, two rape victims killed themselves in response to social media pictures of, and comments about, their rapes while unconscious (Grinberg 2013). College student Elisa Lopez was sexually assaulted on the subway and subsequently traumatized by a creepshot video circulating on the

Internet. She said that she could recover from the attack, but the video wouldn't go away. The video haunted her and made it impossible for her to continue with her life as she had before (Filipovic 2014). This is the case with many of the victims whose sexual assault is circulated or posted on social media. As we've seen, many of them find the public humiliation even more traumatic and upsetting than the sexual assault itself.

In addition to becoming part of the harassment of victims, photographs taken by the perpetrators also can be used against them in court. New apps for cellphones, however, such as Snapchat, where pictures or messages sent around disappear after twenty-four hours, or Yik Yak, where messages disappear, seem designed to circumvent this possibility. But even these apps are bringing to light rapes and victimization that may have remained hidden otherwise. For example, Yik Yak chatting at Stanford revealed that an eighteen-year-old girl, who was unconscious at the time, was raped by a Stanford varsity swimmer, described as "a clean-cut star athlete" and "the all-American boy next door" (Glenza & Carroll 2015). Rumors about the sexual assault circulating on Yik Yak eventually led to an investigation into a crime that might otherwise never have been reported. Social media, then, can serve a complicated double function when it comes to sexual assault and rape. On the one hand, it can be used to further humiliate and harass victims of sexual assault. On the other hand, it can be used to alert authorities to sex crimes and it can provide evidence to try and convict perpetrators.

SOCIAL MEDIA AND THE DENIGRATION OF WOMEN

Arguably, social media such as Facebook, Snapchat, and Tinder were invented as part of a culture that objectifies and denigrates girls and women. It is well known that Facebook founder and

Harvard graduate, Mark Zuckerberg, now one of the richest men in the country, invented the social media site Facebook to post pictures of girls for his college buddies to rate and berate. And it was recently uncovered that Stanford graduate Evan Spiegel, inventor of Snapchat, which is estimated to be worth at least $3 billion, sent messages during his days in a fraternity referring to women as "bitches," "sororisluts," to be "peed on," and discussed getting girls drunk to have sex with them (Hu 2014). The wildly popular hookup site Tinder, with 1.6 billion "swipes" and 26 million matches a day, has changed the way people date (Morgan 2015). Now using proximity sensors, the mobile app allows users to view pictures and swipe right if they like what they see and swipe left if not. If there is a match between two users who swipe right, then they can message each other or "keep playing." Tinder, seeded on college campuses by former University of California students and cofounders Sean Rad and Justin Mateen, has generated new urban slang, "tinderslut," to refer to women who use Tinder to hook up with men. Rad and Mateen faced criticism when they gave the term two emoji thumbs-up on social media. Tinder has also spawned another term for attractive women users, "Tinderella." One of the definitions of Tinderella listed by online Urban Dictionary reads: "A really hot girl on a dating app called Tinder. Sam: Hey Tom, had any luck on Tinder yet? Tom: Dude I got a match with a Tinderella, and I fucked her! Sam: Nice work dude." A YouTube video entitled "Tinderella: A Modern Fairytale" has the caption, "Present day Cinderella doesn't wait for a fairy godmother to fix her up, she uses Tinder. Watch our take on the classic fairytale, updated for 2014. It may not end happily ever after, but it's good enough for tonight."[56]

Both Tinder cofounders are also involved in a sexual harassment suit wherein Mateen is accused of severely and repeatedly harassing the former vice president of marketing for Tinder, Whitney Wolfe, who claims that he sent her harassing sexist messages calling her a "slut," a "gold-digger," and a "whore," along with insulting her in public while Rad watched on and did nothing

(Bercovici 2014). Wolfe also claims that Rad and Mateen refused to name her as a cofounder because she is "a girl." Given the continued use of social media to target, harass, and humiliate young women, it is telling that all of these technologies were born out of sexist attitudes toward women. Facebook and Snapchat were explicitly designed to denigrate women. Many social media sites, like other forms of traditional media, bank on images of attractive girls and women.

It is not just that many popular social media sites were invented by men who enjoyed denigrating women, but also that these social media sites were invented to denigrate women. Facebook was invented to rank women's faces and bodies. Snapchat was invented to talk about women in ways that would disappear so men could avoid later accountability. The same is true of Yik Yak. And, some feminists have argued in mainstream media that Tinder serves the interests of men who want to hook up more than it does of women (Bogle 2008; Frietas 2013). Arguably, Tinder was invented to actualize pornographic fantasies of hooking up with women for sex only without intimacy, if not without intersubjectivity. Given that most social media has an essential visual dimension, photographs that promote what I call elsewhere a "pornographic way of looking" are inherent to the medium (Oliver 2007). Photographs of girls and women looking sexy and cute are the mainstay of some sites, especially creepshot sites.

In creepshots, the lack of consent is essential, as is outlined on websites that specialize in creepshots such as Tumblr's *creepshooter*, *creepshots.com*, and metareddit's *creepshots*. Metareddit's website specifies, "*Creepshots* are CANDID. If a person is posting for and/or aware that a picture is being taken, then it is no longer candid and ceases to be a *creepshot*. A creepshot captures the natural, raw sexiness of the subject. . . . Use stealth, cunning and deviousness to capture the beauty of your unsuspecting, chosen target" ("Creepshots" n.d.). Clearly, girls and women are seen as unsuspecting "targets," prey to be "shot" and "captured" on film. They are cut into pieces, valued for the body parts, anonymously taken from them by the camera and posted online. On all of these creepshot websites, there are subcategories such as "ass," "poop sex," "crouch," "boobs," "jailbait," and "teen."[57]

Some creepshot videos end up on pornographic sites. For example, college student Elisa Lopez was in disbelief when a coworker showed her a video circulating online in which a man was penetrating her with his fingers as she lay passed out on the subway train after partying with friends. Rather than helping her, a bystander took a video and posted it online. Lopez tried without success to get the video taken down. Traumatized by the video, even more than the sexual assault, Lopez became depressed, her schoolwork suffered, and she almost ended up in the mental ward of a hospital. Although getting better, years afterwards, Lopez is still traumatized by the creepshot video (Filipovic 2014). Because of the vigilance of Lopez and her friends, eventually a suspect was arrested for the sexual assault, but not for the creepshot, which damaged Lopez as much, if not more, than the assault (Q13 Fox News Staff 2015).

Creepshots are valued because of the lack of consent on the part of the subject. Her agency is described as "vain attempts at putting on a show for the camera," and thus to be evacuated from the images. Creepshooters are likened to hunters choosing a target. The camera is their weapon. Subjects of creepshots do not give their consent. Indeed, insofar as they are unaware that they are being photographed, they cannot give consent—unless women moving through the world in their everyday activities wearing their everyday clothes (see *yoga pants* as a subcategory of creepshots) constitutes consent. This suggests that women's bodies are public property; or that when women are in public, they are fair game, especially if they are wearing creepshot-worthy clothes. Creepshots display not only the "sexy" girl or her body part but also the hunting prowess of the creeper photographer. The same applies to raping unconscious girls. Their lack of consent is the conquest, documented now through creepshot photographs posted online as trophies. Within this world of creepshots and rape drugs, nonconsensual sex is valued because the lack of consent is considered *hot*.

As became apparent in both the Steubenville and Vanderbilt cases, along with the sexual assaults, taking creepshot photographs of unconscious naked girls or women and distributing them is a crime. In both cases, perpetrators were found guilty not only of rape but also of taking and distributing illegal photographs. In the Steubenville case, perpetrators were charged with distributing child pornography (the victim was only sixteen). In the Vanderbilt case, Brandon Vandenburg's lawyer claimed "all" he was guilty of was taking the photos, and explained the cover-up saying, "at least he had the good sense to be upset afterwards" (20/20 2015). What also became apparent in these cases is that the photographs and videos were an important part of the rape itself. The boys and men smiled and clowned for the camera, joked and jeered for posterity, and took pleasure not only in sexually abusing their victims but also in capturing it on film, and then sharing it with friends. Reportedly, in the Vanderbilt case, Corey Batey told Brandon Vandenburg to "get this on camera," as he raped their unconscious victim.

As we have seen, fraternities around the country have been sanctioned for posting photographs of unconscious naked or semi-clothed women, some in embarrassing sexual positions (Associated Press 2015; Frampton 2015; O'Connell 2015; Robbins 2015). The women involved did not know or consent. Some of these photographs may be evidence of sexual assault or nonconsensual sex, as well as illegal in their own right. Yet as one fraternity member at Penn State University said, "It is a brotherhood and nobody expects anyone to go and post stuff publicly or so forth and so on. It's a real disappointment that this kid went and did this. It was an entirely satirical group and it was funny to some extent. But this is not a criminal thing. It's not anyone else's business, pretty much. It's an interfraternity thing and that's that" (O'Connell 2015). Obviously, these fraternity boys think that pictures of naked women and their body parts, circulated to hundreds on Facebook, is fun and funny, but not criminal. In their eyes, the real crime is that one of their brothers betrayed them by reporting it.

Serial rapists and sexual predators who seek out vulnerable girls, drug them, or prey on intoxicated girls, and then view their rapes as conquests, are increasingly photographing their unconscious victims as a new form of trophy.[58] As the documentary *The Hunting Ground* shows, some of these boys take pleasure in the hunt, see girls as their "prey," and take pictures as trophies. In the film, one fraternity member described sessions where fraternity brothers would report on their sexual exploits to see who had had the most transgressive—or aggressive—sex, wherein anal penetration was most valued. (It is noteworthy that sodomy was a felony in the United States until 1962, and it was still illegal in fourteen states until 2003.) Another fraternity collected photographs of girls' breasts taken by their members (often without consent), and posted them as trophies. While boys bragging about their sexual exploits is not new, posting creepshot pictures of their victims on social media is new, and so is the notion of "nonconsensual sex." The two go hand in hand. In sum, both are symptoms of a valorization of lack of women's consent.

While rape and debasement of women are not new, the use of social media to do so is. The use of ubiquitous cellphone cameras to take creepshots of unsuspecting women, including unconscious rape victims, makes clear that contemporary mainstream youth culture values lack of consent. In other words, it is not just that some men will take pictures or have sex without a woman's consent, but also that photographs are valued more where there is no consent. Moreover, with creepshots, by definition the lack of consent must be obvious. The photograph needs to display the unsuspecting woman or her body parts, along with the fact that she doesn't know that she's being photographed. Of course, this makes an unconscious woman the perfect subject for creepshots. In addition, seeing women in compromising positions, naked, or sexually violated, is considered "funny." Again, while candid camera or humor in humiliating photos has been around since photography itself, so has the penetration of pornographic images into mainstream culture. If men or boys used to secretly share pictures of naked women, now they do so publicly. Whereas, in the past, pornographic pictures were produced for mass consumption but sold privately, even wrapped in brown paper and only to adults, now the Internet is filled with selfie porn, sexting photos, and creepshots of women who are not professionals. Reality television has put an increased value on "realness," even if it is staged realness. Rapists hamming it up for the camera, and taking creepshots of unsuspecting unconscious girls, are part and parcel of the patriarchal pornutopia in the age of social media.

3

GIRLS AS PREDATORS AND PREY

IN RECENT LITERATURE AND FILM, "realness," and the ability to distinguish fantasy from reality, are crucial assets for girls navigating the hyperviolent worlds of Young Adult dystopias. Our tough-girl protagonists need to know what's real and what's not. They don't fall for simulations. They don't get caught up in reality television. They don't pay attention to the cameras recording their lives. They have more important things to worry about than social media, namely, surviving and protecting those they love. As technological advances like the Internet and social media blur the line between fantasy and reality, or perhaps even change our conception of reality, like Tris in *Divergent* or Katniss in *The Hunger Games*, the savvy girl navigating her way into womanhood must learn to distinguish fantasy from reality in order to survive. Even in *Fifty Shades of Grey*, Ana navigates Christian's fantasy sex versus real sex, the sex they have in the bedroom and not in the playroom, the sex that is a form of communication and love. In these three films, girls save their traumatized boys and men from their abusive pasts and offer them real true love by showing them what is real and reversing the effects of past fantasies, or in the case of *Divergent* and *The Hunger Games*, brainwashing by the corrupt authorities. In these contemporary tales, the violent princes are not to blame for assaulting the girls they love. Like their princesses, these boys are victims of corrupt and corrupting cultures that make them hurt the ones they love.

The implicit danger for these girls becoming women is that life is not what it seems: That pretty mother figure with a smile on her face is really plotting her surrogate daughter's demise. Technologies, especially recording technologies, which once promised progress have turned against these girls, threatening them with illusions and exposure. Simulation technologies and reality television have invaded real life to the point that no one is safe from surveillance and manipulation. Even one's deepest fears and desires, or most intimate thoughts or moments, can be recorded, projected on screens, and seen by all. On top of that, their boyfriends may attack at any moment. Those boys are violent, and they have been brainwashed by their corrupt society to want to hurt the girls they love. In light of the real threat of rape in the lives of girls and young women, these films address a fear and a fantasy that runs throughout our culture, the deep-seated and age-old fear and fantasy of rape, now combined with the fear of its broadcast across social media.

Unlike their classic princess predecessors, these girls aren't waiting for a prince to save them. Instead, through their brains and brawn, they are saving themselves and him too. These smart girls don't fall for illusions, simulations, fantasies, or fairytales. In addition to physical strength, these contemporary princesses hold the epistemological trump cards when it comes to distinguishing fiction from reality. They save their violent princes by waking them up to reality. They show their beloved boys what's real and what's fantasy; and by so doing, they transform these traumatized boys from brainwashed brutes into loving partners. Peeta (*The Hunger Games*) and Four (*Divergent*) have been programmed by the powers that be and that is why they are attacking their girlfriends. Their abusive attitudes toward girls are not just the result of individual psychology, but rather of both personal and systematic abuse. These boys are products of high-tech cultures that program them to debase and abuse the girls they love. Damaged by systems of oppression, they too are victims caught up in beliefs beyond their control. If rape culture is to blame for rape, then these boys are products of that culture rather than its beneficiaries. It is up to the girls to teach them to trust instead of fight and assault those they love. In this Young Adult fantasy, potentially violent boys can be redeemed through tough love—and an occasional knee to the groin.

Perhaps we can forge a link between recent testimony from young men in the Vanderbilt rape case and these boys who disclaim responsibility for their own violence, especially toward their girlfriends. Like Peeta and Four, at their trial Brandon Vandenberg and Corey Batey claimed they were not responsible for what they did. They said they didn't recognize themselves in the photographs and videos, and that this behavior was not who they *really* are. When sober, they suggested they would never behave this way. Their lawyers blamed it on the party culture on campus. They argued that their clients too were victims of the party culture on campus, but that isn't real. These young men aren't rapists. In reality, they suggested, they are fine upstanding young men, athletes with bright futures. Perhaps like Peeta and Four, they claim to have been brainwashed by a culture that exploits their violence and redirects it toward the very ones they love. They too claim to have been traumatized by the experience of the assault, traumatized by their own violence against women. In the Vanderbilt case, given that two of the accused were convicted, spent months in jail, and now face another trial, they probably do regret their actions. They probably are traumatized by the experience of expulsion from school, promising careers a memory, felony crime convictions, living in jail, and public awareness of their crimes. But unlike Peeta and Four, their abused victim will not redeem their violence—although Vandenberg did try to enlist the victim to help to cover up the assault. He sent her loving messages and treated her with extra kindness after the attack: so much so, that, not knowing what really happened, she apologized to him.

Traumatized and exposed, like the victims of creepshot recording, our filmic Young Adult heroes and heroine's fears and desires are projected onto the big screen for all to see. Vulnerable and beaten, bruised and bloodied, spectators both inside and outside of the filmic narratives watch these boys and girls suffering for entertainment. Part of what makes them strong, however, is that these girls aren't afraid of exposing themselves. They have bigger things on their minds than whether or not a video of them kissing, or fighting, or half-clothed, has gone viral. We see independent girls who don't care what anyone thinks, making their own way in a violent world. These tough girls seemingly provide new role models for fighting back. And yet, they are continually punished for fighting back. These hunting, hunted girls are both predators and prey. They are both brutal and brutalized. In these contemporary fairytales, for the first time we see fiercely independent, strong smart girls who are agents of their own lives; but at the same time, as never before, we see teenage girls beaten almost to death, for displaying such pluck.

In the age of social media, these girls may not have any secrets safe from public scrutiny, but they are not fooled by the illusions screened all around them. They navigate the world of social media and learn to use it to their advantage. In *The Hunger Games*, the Capitol watches as Katniss fights for her life and hidden cameras film her first kiss. Her every move is under surveillance. In *Divergent*, Tris's desires and fears are no longer her own; they are projected onto screens for all to see. These girls play for the cameras when necessary, but don't get caught up in their own humiliation for long, even when their most intimate and candid moments are broadcast for all to see. They get over it. Within the dystopic narratives of Young Adult futuristic fantasies, these smart hunting girls, predators and prey, smash the apparatus of ideological mythmaking to become the heroines of their own stories. Stepping outside of these narratives, we see new myths of strong girls who overcome the odds in a violent world, girls who fight off, and fight for, the boys they love. The new fairytale princesses may be beaten, and even raped, but they are not going to allow social media to further traumatize them. They have already been stripped naked for all the world to see, their families have been killed, their bodies subjected to pain and torture. What more can harm them? Not social media.

This fantasy of fighting back against the violence of the transition from girlhood to womanhood, which is fraught with both the thrills of sexual awakening and the threat of sexual assault, requires becoming immune to the harms of social media. At a time when in the world outside of film, social media is further traumatizing rape victims, when photographs or videos of unconscious girls being abused can go viral, these filmic fantasies give us girls whose trauma and brutalization is caught on film for all to see, and yet doesn't touch them. In fact, it is social media that turns the tide in *The Hunger Games*. The Capitol's use of "reality television" backfires when sympathy for Katniss sparks a revolution. Videos intended to humiliate and entertain become evidence of abuse that humanizes rather than humiliates its victims. Both inside and outside of these narratives, while some find videos of teenagers abusing each other amusing, others see them as evidence of a corrupt culture in need of revolution.

These Young Adult fantasies hit the mark in terms of showing how social media can both entertain and spark revolution. In real life, photographs and videos of unconscious girls being sexually assaulted are posted to social media to further humiliate victims and entertain perpetrators. Yet these same photographs and videos become evidence of brutal assault and the hostile or flippant attitudes of perpetrators. Like the videos of Katniss in *The Hunger Games*, photographs and videos of teenage girls being abused are becoming the catalyst for changing attitudes toward rape victims. The photos themselves are being used to distinguish fiction from reality. At the same time that these photographs, the descriptions of them, and their very existence are evidence of a valorization of lack of consent and continued sexual objectification of girls and women, they also show the reality of an abusive culture in need of change.

In many ways, popular dystopic coming-of-age stories are feminist revenge fantasies. But they are complicated revenge fantasies that work to make these girls both predators and prey. Their fearlessness and ferocity come from their loss and trauma. They are survivors. They are assaulted, fight back, and move on. These girls are avenging the wrongs done to them. Yet their brutalization can be interpreted as retaliation for their strength and independence. It can be read as retaliation against their postfeminist attempts to write their own fates. Just as in the real world girls and women receive retaliation and threats when they fight back against assault and violence, so too do the girls in these fantasy worlds. Within the fantasy worlds, perhaps too often like the real world, violence is always met with violence, and our heroines barely survive. Young women and teenage girls as protagonists saving the world may be something new, but watching girls and women being beaten and raped is not. Still, within these narratives, puberty and the transition to womanhood is the source not only of danger and violence but also of knowledge and power. These smart girls have the power to distinguish truth from fiction, reality from fairytale. These savvy girls are not going to fall into the trap of waiting for a prince to save them. When these girls say "no," they mean it. Anyone who doesn't believe them is going to learn the hard way.

Given the astounding numbers of girls and young women who are sexually assaulted, it is easy to understand the popularity of the fantasy of tough filmic heroines who can fight back. Whereas in their everyday lives, girls and young women face violence, especially sexual violence, these strong no-nonsense film heroines give us fantasies of girls who not only resist gender stereotypes but also "give as good as they get." The problem is that they still get as much, or more, than they give. As we have seen, filmic representations of violence toward girls anesthetize their abuse in ways that not only normalize violence, including sexual violence, but also valorize it. These films send double messages. On the one hand, they give us heroines for whom "no" means don't try it or you'll get hurt. On the other, they delight in violence toward girls, as if abuse is a normal part of coming-of-age. Unfortunately, it is all too true that violence and abuse are part of the lives of girls and young women. Yet reveling in the assault of girls and young women on film works to further normalize violence toward girls even as it gives us fantasies of feminist avengers who fight against it.

FROM PRINCESS TO HUNTRESS

With the avid and expert bow-hunting character of Katniss Everdeen, the Artemis figure has become the new icon of girl power. Several recent blockbuster Hollywood films feature teenage girls hunting and killing animals (*Hanna*, *Winter's Bone*, *The Hunger Games*, *Twilight: Breaking Dawn–Part 2*). Even Disney (and other animated) princesses have become hunters, especially in the persona of the feisty bow-and-arrow shooting princess Merida in *Brave*, who uses her bow to compete for her own hand in marriage and make her own fate (2012). These films feature girls that demonstrate their fortitude and no-nonsense attitudes by hunting animals. But what does it mean that Hollywood's latest girl protagonists are more comfortable in the forest chasing animals than they are among their high school peers? How has Hollywood gone from Disney princesses who have a special bond with their animal friends, to these Artemis figures wielding bows and arrows to take down their animal prey? And why are these girls also being hunted? Although the main female characters are not killed, they are beaten and subjected to violence. They are both hunters and prey. How should we interpret these representations of strong girls who are also abused? What is the relationship between their hunting animals and their being hunted? In this chapter, I argue that these fantasies of hunting, hunted girls are retellings of familiar coming-of-age fairytales, only adapted for a contemporary audience. In this regard, like all fairytales, they warn of the dangers of the transition from girlhood to womanhood, while promising the possibility of overcoming those dangers in triumph. Whereas in classic fairytales, Prince Charming overcomes the dangers in order to vanquish the princess or sweep her off her feet, in these contemporary versions the girls are doing the vanquishing and their feet are firmly planted on the ground.

Images of hunting girls in Hollywood films can be interpreted as adaptations of classic fairytales such as Cinderella, Sleeping Beauty, Beauty and the Beast, and the Little Mermaid. In more or less explicit ways, these popular films repeat and reform themes from familiar fairytales. Some traditional characteristics are retained, such as beauty, innocence, virginity, and an uncanny connection to nature. New elements are added, such as hunting prowess, fearlessness, violent tendencies, and a fighting spirit. The hostile forces traditionally personified by an evil witch, wicked stepmother, or an abusive father are associated with corrupt adult authority figures, which, like their predecessors, often figure as bad parental surrogates.[1] But rather than cruel individuals exploiting our princess as in Cinderella or Sleeping Beauty, these girls are being exploited by a society that has been corrupted. Instead of whistling while they work, our contemporary heroines are traumatized by their experiences and show all the signs of post-traumatic stress disorder, including anxiety, nightmares, day sweats, and hallucinations. Even the adults who should keep them safe can't be trusted. Both modern-day princesses and princes are survivors, victims of abuse, who continue to suffer from PTSD. In contemporary Young Adult fantasies, the princess's struggles do not (always) center on finding her prince. As often as not, she is rescuing him rather than the other way around. Still, for the most part, these new narratives of strong girls overcoming the forces of evil to live somewhat happily—if traumatized—ever after, are circumscribed within the familiar story of heterosexual romance, at least in part, or in the end. They trade on the abuse and battery of their young heroines, within the narratives of the film for the perverse pleasure of adults, and outside for our viewing pleasure. If Sleeping Beauty and its fairytale sisters are tales of exploitation and rape, then these contemporary fairytales continue this line, even as our new princesses are fighting back and struggling to determine and assert their own desires.

It is telling that in the James Bond send-up, Kingsman: The Secret Service (2015), the gentleman spy espousing "manners maketh man" saves the princess of Sweden, Tilde, from the dungeon and asks for a kiss in exchange. She responds that she'll give him "a lot more than that," and asks if they can "do it in the asshole." When Eggsy, the teenage spy, returns, Princess Tilde is waiting for him, lounging on a bed, "sunnyside up." Obviously, we are a long way from Disney, when princesses are taking it up the ass and liking it. Certainly, Disney princesses have had to adapt to changing times and women's changing roles. Given the power these princesses have over the imaginations of young children, especially little girls, they not only mirror social change and expectations for girls and women but also produce desires, fears, and ideals for generations of girls. In a sense, these fairytales, especially as projected onto the big screen and, in most cases, replayed countless times on little screens at home or on the road, form our cultural unconscious. For better or worse, these images are burned into our very souls.

Disney princesses have changed over the years to accommodate changing attitudes toward gender roles.[2] Early Disney princesses like Snow White (1937), Cinderella (1950), and Sleeping Beauty (1959) were demure and feminine; they waited for a prince to rescue them from their ordinary lives, a prince whose love and charm would transform them into a princess. These girls were subservient to their overbearing guardians. They got by with their beauty alone. These princesses were part of a culture in which women had gained political rights, particularly voting rights (with the 19th Amendment in 1920), but still lacked social equality, or financial and sexual independence.[3]

Decades later, Team Disney's princesses were still waiting to be transported by love, but they were a bit pluckier and quite a bit sexier, including *The Little Mermaid* (1989), *Beauty and the Beast* (1991), Jasmine in *Aladdin* (1992), *Pocahontas* (1995), and *Mulan* (1998).[4] These princesses reflected changing attitudes toward women's activities and social status. No longer just beautiful, they were also active. They didn't simply wait for their princes; they actively pursued a different lifestyle. They had personalities that included intelligence, bravery, stubbornness, wisdom, and took us well beyond the beautiful girl waiting in the tower for her prince to take her away on his white horse. In addition, by incorporating ethnically diverse heroines, these films responded to criticisms of second wave feminism that it was white and middle class, ignoring the concerns of women of color and lower or working-class women. These princesses dreamt of a better life and actively pursued it. Yet, in large part, that better life was still defined in terms of a heterosexual marriage to a prince. And many of these girls made sacrifices for his sake. The most extreme case is Ariel, who gives up her voice to be with her true love.

More recently, both Disney and DreamWorks have given us more assertive and physically stronger princesses. With *Shrek*'s princess Fiona (2001), *Brave*'s princess Merida (2012), and *Frozen*'s Anna and Elsa (2013), we have active, even athletic princesses, who enter a man's world as equals.[5] Princess Merida shuns her suitors, preferring to win her own hand using her archery skills so that she can continue to spend her free time in the forest riding her horse, shooting arrows, and hunting (although we only see her kill a salmon to feed her queen mother, who has been turned into a bear by an inept witch). With *Brave*, even the youngest audiences are served an Artemis-style princess who prefers hunting to boys.

FIGURE 3.1 Merida in *Brave* (2012), directed by Brenda Chapman and Mark Andrews.

In *Frozen*, younger sister Princess Anna's fairytale fantasy of marrying a prince becomes a nightmare when the prince turns out to be a corrupt and abusive opportunist. Her older sister Elsa shuns boys altogether, and in the end rules the kingdom on her own. Maleficent too learns the hard way that boys can't be trusted when Stephan drugs and dismembers her.

From early Disney princesses, through tongue-in-cheek send-ups of those princesses in *Shrek* and *Enchanted* (2007), all of these girls keep company with animals that figure as important companions, friends, and even kin. Even while their personalities, appearance, dress, and activities change, their kinship with animals is something that doesn't change over the decades. Like their live-action counterparts in films such as *The Wizard of Oz* (1939), *National Velvet* (1944), *Andre* (1994), *Whale Rider* (2002), *Nim's Island* (2008), and *Avatar* (2009), these girls have special bonds with animals. One way to interpret these girls' closeness to animals is that traditionally girls and women have been seen as akin to animals, or at least closer to their animal instincts than men. These girls have a special relationship to nature. They are part of nature, as evidenced by their kinship with animals. This kinship with animals and nature also signals their innocence. In fairytales, nature is good, and girls' kinship with it, or power over it, protects them.

Like nature itself, however, these girls' special relationship with nature is seen as threatening. Nature represents both innocence and purity as well as danger and unimaginable horrors. Various horror films capitalize on this animalistic connection between women and animals, films in which women turn into animals, usually sexual predators—for example, *Cat People* (1942), *She-Wolf of London* (1946), *The Wasp Woman* (1959), and more recently *The Brood* (1979), and *Species* (1995), among others. One recent film, *Splice* (2010), is noteworthy because it features a pubescent girl creature who is a genetically engineered human-animal hybrid named Dren; she enters puberty, has sex with her human "father" and then kills him, changes her own sex and then rapes and impregnates her human "mother." Before she becomes sexually mature, Dren kills a rabbit and eats it raw, to the horror of her vegetarian mother; and she befriends a kitten that she later kills as a sort of revenge on her human mother. Dren is portrayed as more animal than human, especially insofar as her human mother doesn't fully acknowledge Dren's humanity. Dren is capable of love, which she expresses toward her kitten. And yet, she is capable of great violence, which she also expresses toward her cat and other animals, including humans. Dren embodies the hunting, hunted girl, both predator and prey, who becomes violent in the face of violence. For it is after a particularly horrific scene of symbolic castration-rape, where her mother cuts off her tail, that Dren fully embraces the violence within her. Dren is *made* violent by her messed-up parents, who are themselves traumatized and victims of violence. In true horror film fashion, Dren gets her revenge by raping her mother and killing her father.

Recent Hollywood blockbusters featuring strong girls hunting and killing animals leaves us with the question of how to explain this move from girls loving, or being, animals to girls hunting and killing animals. Is this move to represent girls as tougher and more self-sufficient feminist progress or yet another patriarchal fantasy? Certainly, fairytales need to adapt to current gender norms. Yet these bloodthirsty teens killing game large and small, along with other people—or in the case of *Twilight*'s Bella, vampires—seem to go beyond gender parity at the movies. Moreover, their popularity indicates that these nervy girls have hit a nerve. Both the *Twilight* films and *The Hunger Games* are among the top-grossing films in history; and both have held the place as biggest box office hit ever; *Twilight* held the spot until *The Hunger Games* eclipsed its sales.

Why do we find violent pubescent girls killing animals, humans, and the occasional vampire, so appealing? Is this equal-opportunity killing? Perhaps these are feminist revenge fantasies, cute and sexy girls with arrows and guns giving it back to "the man." Or perhaps recent films present us with beaten, bloodied, and abused girls as punishment for their fighting back. In either case, these films work to normalize violence both by and against girls and young women. Furthermore, animals become the sacrificial lambs and scapegoats for patriarchal culture that debases women and girls. Killing, instead of loving, animals has become the emblem of girl power. Just as girls are hunted and attacked with relish in these films, our heroines displace that patriarchal violence onto their animal prey. In these hunting fantasies, empowerment is seen as much in terms of violence as any other form of resistance. As we will see, these images of tough girls take us back to classic myths of femininity even while they signal a new level of violence by and toward girls. New myths of Artemis figures defending their own virtue from the violence all around them can be interpreted as compensatory fantasies for girls and young women subjected to violence, especially sexual violence, in their everyday lives. If the contemporary world is a violent place for girls and young women, as these contemporary fairytales warn, our new kick-ass heroines aren't going to take it lying down. Bloodied and bruised, they will go out fighting.

HANNA: THE LITTLE MERMAID

The protagonist in *Hanna* is the sixteen-year-old girl for whom the film is named. Raised by her rogue CIA agent father (Eric Bana) in an isolated arctic forest, Hanna (Saorise Ronan) has learned not only to be self-sufficient but also to speak several languages, operate complicated weaponry, and to kill.

The film opens with Hanna hunting a caribou in a tense chase scene that ends with the animal falling, moaning and gasping its last breath in close-up. As the film progresses, we learn that Hanna's mother was part of a CIA experiment run by Marissa Weigler (Cate Blanchett), who convinced pregnant women who wanted abortions to participate in a study that enhanced their fetuses with heightened intelligence, strength, agility, and tolerance for violence. On her sixteenth birthday, Erik presents Hanna with a box-shaped device adorned with a big red button. He tells her that once she presses the button, Marissa Weigler will find them and he can no longer protect her; she will have to leave their forest hideout and enter civilization so that she can kill Weigler.

FIGURE 3.2 Hanna (Saorise Ronan) in *Hanna* (2011), directed by Joe Wright.

Like the Little Mermaid, Hanna longs to emerge from her secluded forest and see the world of real girls. Actress Soarise Ronan, who plays Hanna, says, "The structure of the story is basically . . . about a girl who's lived in the castle her whole life and suddenly she breaks out and is introduced to evil and beauty and ugliness and all these different things . . . The Little Mermaid who is breaking to the surface and wants to be a real girl" (qtd. in Rosenberg 2011). The centerpiece of the film is a wide-eyed Hanna experiencing the human world for the first time, including making friends with another teenaged girl, Sophie, who tells her about makeup and boys. But she also discovers that the world is a dangerous, even cruel place where she doesn't belong. Director Joe Wright describes Hanna as the Little Mermaid who discovers that the real world is cruel: "The Little Mermaid is the story of Hanna. The idea that she grows up under the surface and imagines the world above as this beautiful, romantic place. And of course she gains legs and they are painful, and she discovers the world is quite cruel" (qtd. in Greco 2011). While at the end of the film Hanna is alone in the real world without friend or family, in the screenplay she goes back to her isolated forest cabin to find her fox puppy waiting for her. This original ending suggests not only that this is where Hanna belongs (not in the real world) but also that her real family may be the animals with whom she shares the forest, perhaps even the ones she eats.

Rather than living under the sea and wishing for legs so that she can walk on land, Hanna lives in the forest close to animals but longs to join the human world. For her, the tension between the under and over worlds becomes the tension between nature and technology, heightened by the fact that Hanna herself is created through both. She is a genetically engineered child designed to kill—we might say, designed to kill *like an animal* without remorse. Hanna, like other girls in recent films running through the forest, represents the innocence of nature. Yet her innocence is also threatening when "unleashed" on society. Like a predatory animal, she is both innocent and dangerous. Her hunting prowess gives her the edge when fleeing and fighting her pursuers. Like many animals, she is both predator and prey. She not only hunts, she is also being hunted. While in the case of men, their hunting animals might be seen as proving men's superiority to, or dominion over, other animals, in the case of these girls, hunting brings them even closer to animals. Hanna feels more comfortable in the world of animals than in the world of humans. (Indeed, the original screenplay has her leave civilization to go back to the world of the animals where a fox cub is her only companion.) Aside from training her to kill men, her hunting skills appear superfluous, even inappropriate, in civilized society, as evidenced in a scene where she throws a freshly skinned rabbit on the breakfast table of her newly found friend's campsite and the whole family is disgusted.

In *Hanna*, there is nostalgia for the natural world untouched by technology. Hanna and her father live in a world both before and beyond technology. Aside from Hanna's strict and demanding training routine, they have an idyllic life. It is only when her father digs up the locator beacon with the ominous big red button that their peaceful life turns into a deadly nightmare. Technology interrupts nature and brings chaos to the seeming natural order of things. While the film later leaves Hanna alone, mourning her father and stranded in the human world, the screenplay places her back where she belongs, living simply within the natural chain of being, hunting some animals and befriending others.

How is it that nostalgia for lost natural habitat and the loss of innocence go together in these films? Do these girls represent the lost innocence of nature, now corrupted by technologies of destruction? Their position on the cusp between childhood and womanhood seems threatening, perhaps more threatening than the fully mature femme fatale, precisely because of their innocence. In other words, there is something attractive about these pubescent warriors who bring together fantasies of innocence, innocence lost, and phallic women shooting arrows and guns. They are more dangerous because we don't expect them to be violent gun- or arrow-slinging "tough guys." They look as innocent as kittens, but their claws do more damage. If these girls are particularly menacing because they don't look dangerous, that is in part because stereotypes of girls, as evidenced in their Disney predecessors, play on their supposed passivity, helplessness, and pure hearts. While our new princess warriors may still have good hearts, they may not be as pure as they once were.

These dangerous girls signal anxieties about lost innocence along with the excitement of that loss, represented not only by the move from nature to high-tech culture but also by the loss of virginity and the loss of purity. In these films, technology and loss of virginity come together, as if it were technology that deflowers the girls at the same time that it introduces them to the thrilling yet cruel world of adult sexuality. These girls' transition to womanhood is paralleled by the transition from nature to culture, specifically to a highly technological world. As they move out of the forest and into society, they begin to experience their (human) sexuality as a new technologically mediated danger. In different ways in all of these films featuring hunting girls (*Hanna*, *Avatar*, *Twilight*, and *The Hunger Games*), human sexuality replaces or supplements animal sexuality. The innocent yet erotic relationship that the girls have with the forest and the animals in it gives way to a more properly, and more dangerous, human sexuality. Still, in *Hanna* and *The Hunger Games* in particular, the girls' interest in animals and the call of the wild is always in tension with their interest in boys and the tug of civilized society. Indeed, their closeness to animals, even when—or especially when—hunting represents the joy of youth, while the lure of kissing boys signals their transition to womanhood. While this lure is a curiosity for them, they also remain wedded to their earlier pleasures in the forest with animals. Indeed, the world of boys and kisses is an even more dangerous world—not only for these girls but also for the boys brave enough to try it. As if warning of possible sexual assault from those closest to them, these coming-of-age fantasies suggest sexual violence even while warding it off through our heroine's abilities to defend herself. In addition, in a world saturated by social media and Tinder taking over sexual relations among teens and young adults, technology, specifically media technology, in these films signals not only a loss of innocence, but the dangers of coming of age in the high-tech world.

The *New York Times*'s film critics A. O. Scott and Manohla Dargis suggest that Hanna's training and killer instincts may be a way of keeping her chaste as well as safe: "In 'Hanna' the teenage heroine, raised in arctic isolation by her father, experiences her first kiss and then executes a swift, complex series of martial arts moves on her unsuspecting beau, who winds up flat on his back, gasping for breath. Hanna's finely tuned, self-protective reflexes, drilled into her over the years by her C.I.A.-renegade daddy, have overridden her amorous impulses. Is that a byproduct of the training, or part of a patriarchal program to keep her chaste as well as safe?" (Scott and Dargis 2011). Unlike the other tough-girl protagonists in recent films, Hanna does not get the boy; and more to the point, no boy gets her. She has been trained to defend herself. Hanna will not be the victim of sexual assault. Instinctively, as if sensing danger, she attacks the boy who tries to kiss her. This girl has been trained to be suspicious of all men, and to fight off any sexual instinct with what is much stronger in her, namely, the killer instinct. In light of increasing concerns about rape culture and sexual violence, which is too much part of coming-of-age for high school girls and young college women, Hanna's home-schooling in self-defense and offensive warfare can be seen as not just protecting her chastity but also protecting her from sexual assault. The trade-off, however, is that she ends up alone, a misfit in a world that she doesn't understand. Like the Little Mermaid in Hans Christian Anderson's story (rather than Disney's happy ending), Hanna ends up sacrificing herself to avenge her parents. Hanna succeeds in avenging her mother's death—and her father's—but at what cost to herself? The shining high-tech world she longed to see turns out to be even crueler than the harsh arctic wilderness she left behind.

THE HUNGER GAMES' KATNISS: CINDERELLA

Like *Hanna*, *The Hunger Games* opens with a scene of a girl in a forest chasing an animal; this time it is Katniss Everdeen (Jennifer Lawrence) hunting a deer. Katniss is an avid hunter who survives, and wins, the Hunger Games through her prowess with a bow and arrow and her experience navigating the forest. During the Hunger Games competition, she manages to hunt to eat and feed her new-found friend Rue. In the book, Katniss describes snaring a rabbit that she takes back to cook for Rue during the Games: "I'm about to take off when I think of my snares. Maybe it's imprudent to check them with the others so close. But I have to. Too many years of hunting, I guess. And the lure of possible meat. I'm rewarded with one fine rabbit. In no time, I've cleaned and gutted the animal, leaving the head, feet, tail, skin, and innards, under a pile of leaves." In terms of hunting, the books are far more graphic than the films.

More than the other hunting girls in recent films, Katniss lives to hunt. Throughout Suzanne Collins's *Hunger Games* trilogy, Katniss is constantly dreaming of getting back into the forest to track game. She is happiest when she is on the scent of her prey. She kills animals large and small—mostly small—to survive and to feed her family, at least in the beginning. She describes the wood as "our savoir, and each day I went a bit farther into its arms" (Collins 2010:51). But even after she wins the Hunger Games and her family receives all of the bounty they could ever hope for, she continues to hunt and still thinks of almost nothing else. In the subsequent novels, Katniss negotiates hunting privileges in exchange for serving as the Mockingjay, a mascot for the revolution. She is identified with an animal—or more accurately with a bird—and like a bird of prey, she craves the hunt and the kill. Since her family doesn't need food, she brings game to those who do; and eventually, she supplies meat to the rebel kitchen. Discussing her role as Katniss in *The Hunger Games* movies, Jennifer Lawrence says, "Whenever Gary [Ross, the director] and I would talk about

Katniss, it was '[You're from] District 12 and you're a hunter.'
I didn't feel like an action star, I didn't feel like a superhero. I felt like
a hunter . . . she's a 16-year-old girl who happens to be great with
her senses" (Valby 2013:30). The essence of Katniss is huntress.

As in *Hanna*, there is a sharp juxtaposition between the innocent animal world of the forest and the high-tech human world. In
The Hunger Games, the decadence of human culture and advanced
technologies are manifest in the Capitol, where people alter their
bodies in grotesque ways by using the latest technologies and where
the Hunger Games create technological replicas of the forest and of
animals that threaten rather than reassure. The worst tortures of
the Hunger Games tournament are genetically engineered, or technologically enhanced, hybrid creatures that are far more deadly than
anything in nature. Indeed, in the film and more so in the books,
nature offers Katniss her only respite from both the poverty of her
pre-Games life in District 12 and the technological nightmares of
the Capitol and the Games. In the third book in the series, *Mockingjay*, Katniss discovers an additional district, thirteen, the seat of the
revolution against the Capitol; District 13 is entirely underground
and fully mechanized. Again, there is a stark contrast between the
expansive freedom of the forest and the claustrophobic world of District 13, which is why Katniss insists on the privilege of leaving the
underground bunker to hunt in the forest. Finally, Katniss's victories
along with her beatings are captured by surveillance technologies,
which seem to be everywhere, even in the most intimate spaces. And
yet, it is when her most candid and intimate moments are broadcast
for all to see that Katniss is the most effective. Her makeshift burial
of Rue and her tender kisses shared with Peeta have an emotional
impact that the Capitol can't control, which is how Katniss becomes
the Mockingjay and the inspiration for rebellion in the districts.

Like *Hanna*, *The Hunger Games* exhibits both nostalgia for
natural innocence and anxiety over technological sophistication.
The forest is a place where Katniss is safe, even on her own. It is a
place where she can survive. The Capitol, on the other hand, is a
dangerous place with booby-traps, genetically engineered killers,

and surveillance around every corner. If the innocence of nature is represented by Katniss's own sexual innocence and her sweetness toward her younger sister, then the threat of technology is represented by the ugly "muttations," genetically engineered attack dogs, which nearly shred Katniss in the games. Within the film itself, the "Hunger Games" is a highly technological and deadly reality television program broadcast throughout the districts in order to keep them under control by the Capitol. During the Games, and even outside of the games, every aspect of contestants' lives are recorded and disseminated. Nothing is safe from the prying camera of the Capitol. Every intimate emotion and tender scene, every gory battle or bloodied body, is entertainment for a perverse culture that revels in the pain and sorrow of others. In *The Hunger Games*, life is a spectacle and the dangers of coming-of-age are broadcast live. Reminiscent of cellphone recordings of assaulted unconscious girls, within the narrative of the books and films, bloodied bodies are dragged, unconscious bodies are abused, and images of "dead girls" become entertainment. In the persona of Katniss, the battered girl becomes a cultural icon.

It is interesting that Jennifer Lawrence played another teenage huntress, Ree Dolly, caring for her family in the Ozark Mountains in *Winter's Bone* (2010). In that film, she hunts, kills, and skins squirrels to feed herself and her younger siblings. When asked about PETA's condemnation of the squirrel-skinning scene, reportedly Jennifer Lawrence said, "I should probably say that it wasn't a real squirrel, but screw P.E.T.A" (qtd. in Finn 2015). Like other hunting girls, Ree is also hunted and badly beaten by criminal elements involved with her drug-dealer father. Like Katniss in *The Hunger Games*, Ree in *Winter's Bone* has to look after her siblings because her mother is mentally and emotionally unavailable and her father is missing and then dead.[6] Yet both Katniss and Ree are particularly well served by their hunting skills, taught to them by their fathers. Katniss's training on animals comes in handy when she has to kill people.

Like the lovely close-ups of Hanna's face, shots of our fresh-faced heroine Katniss seem jarring juxtaposed with violent fight scenes, especially those in which these teenage girls are beaten, battered, and bruised. One movie poster for *The Hunger Games* shows a close-up of Katniss with a split lip, scratches on her cheek, and a black eye. Another shows her split in two, one half princess with tiara and gown, the other half in her hunting clothes with bruises on her face. Here again, a princess is being beaten. These movie posters valorize and normalize battered girls. Given the prevalence of domestic abuse of girls and women, these posters evoke real-world violence toward girls. Like the ads mentioned in the introduction, both posters are highly stylized, with pouting (now split) lips, and staring eyes giving "dead smize."

Like Hanna, Katniss is a virgin who has never been kissed. For both, the transition from the forest into the high-tech world parallels their violent transition from girlhood to womanhood. And both have their first kiss on the run from those who want to kill them: Hanna is running from deadly CIA operatives; and Katniss is running from the "career" contestants in the games, the favorites to win. For Katniss, as with Hanna, the first kiss is a complicated event that confuses our heroine with ambivalent desires. For Hanna, her killer instincts become entangled with her sexual desires and she throws her suitor to the ground. While Katniss's first kiss may seem more traditionally romantic, it is vexed by the publicity of the games that motivates it. Although Peeta, the recipient of the kiss, is in love with Katniss, she is only pretending to be in love with him on instructions from her coach in order to get the sympathy of the audience. Part of the narrative of the film and the books is that Katniss herself doesn't always know why she is kissing Peeta. Does she kiss him merely for show or does she love or desire him?

As the story progresses, brainwashed by the Capitol, Peeta turns on Katniss and tries to kill her. As in *Twilight* and *Divergent*, Katniss's boyfriend is dangerous, especially to her. Evoking the image of sixteen-year-old model Hailey Clauson being strangled in *Pop* magazine, or a scene in *The Girl with the Dragon Tattoo* where protagonist Lisbeth Sanders is choked, or the scene in which Hit Girl is beaten and choked unconscious by a mafia boss, or perhaps even a scene from snuff pornography, Peeta tries to strangle Katniss when he first returns from the Capitol. All of these images repeat the theme of a girl being strangled. They focus in on the look of fear in her eyes as she tries to escape her would-be murderer or sexual predator. These violent images show girls and women subject to their worst nightmare, suffocating attacks that threaten their lives. For Katniss, this attack comes from her would-be boyfriend, one of the people closest to her.

Katniss is torn between two potential mates—her hunting pal Gale and her fellow District 12 Hunger Games tribute Peeta. The love triangle theme is a mainstay of tween lit aimed at girls. As in *The Twilight Saga*, the female protagonist must decide between two boys who love her. Unlike Bella in *Twilight*, however, Katniss's world does not revolve around either boy. To the contrary, she is never sure that she is attracted to either one of them. She is always sure that she prefers hunting in the forest and chasing animals to chasing boys. In the end (of the book trilogy), she chooses the baker boy over the hunter because, as she says, "what I need to survive is not Gale's fire, kindled with rage and hatred. I have plenty of fire myself. What I need is the dandelion in the spring. The bright yellow that means rebirth instead of destruction. The promise that life can go on, no matter how bad our losses. That it can be good again. And only Peeta can give me that" (Collins 2014:388). What drives Katniss to Peeta is the same thing that drives her to the forest and to hunt: survival. She needs his hope and optimism to go on. And perhaps she also needs some good bread to go with her rabbit, venison, and squirrel meat.

Like a dystopic Cinderella, in the course of *The Hunger Games* films, and first and second volumes of the trilogy, Katniss goes from rags to riches. As the winner of the Hunger Games, she becomes a celebrity who is lavished with riches. Like Cinderella, Katniss grows up among the ashes. In her case, it is the ash of the coalmines that are the staple of District 12 and in which her father was killed in an explosion. By the opening of the third book in the trilogy, she stands among the ashes of her former life, which was burned to ash by firebombs from the Capitol. Indeed, the title of

FIGURE 3.3 Katniss Everdeen beaten and bloody in *The Hunger Games.*

part one of that book is "The Ashes," and there are fan fiction pieces called *Ash* and *Beneath the Ashes.* Katniss, the girl covered in coal dust, becomes the girl on fire, only later to discover her entire world has been burned. Like Cinderella, Katniss is pulled from the ashes of her world by the love of her "prince," who in this dark fairytale needs her for survival as much as she needs him.

FIGURE 3.4 Katniss as reality television princess.

FIGURE 3.5 Katniss as expert archer.

Indeed, rather than the traditional fairytale in which Cinderella is rescued from the ash pile by the handsome prince, Katniss comes to his rescue many times during the Hunger Games. She chooses the baker Peeta over Gale because she needs rebirth—the Mockingjay becomes a phoenix, who can rise from the ashes renewed no matter how badly burned.

FIGURE 3.6 Brainwashed by the Capitol, Peeta chokes Katniss.

TWILIGHT'S BELLA: BEAUTY AND THE BEAST

Of all of these animal-hunting animalesque girls, Bella Swan (Kristen Stewart) of *The Twilight Saga* comes the closest to being an animal. By the end of the series after Edward turns her into a vampire, she becomes like an animal in that she hunts, kills, and eats (or drinks) other animals with her bare hands and bared teeth. Paradoxically, her vampire body is not an animal body; in leaving behind her human body, she leaves behind the mortal animal body that gets tired, needs sleep, and eventually dies. She becomes an immortal with crystals in her veins instead of blood. Yet, like an animal, her sense of smell is heightened to the point that she can smell the blood of other animals and track their scent. Although as a vampire Bella does not have a living breathing body, all of her senses have become more acute.

It is noteworthy that Kristen Stewart, who plays Bella in *Twilight,* starred in a reboot of the Snow White story, *Snow White and the Huntsman* (2012). In that film, the huntsman sent to kill her rescues Snow White from a deadly forest. In this dark remake of the classic story, Snow White is surrounded by threatening violence in a story told in black, gray, and blood-red. While it is unclear whether Snow White and the huntsman form a romantic couple, she does kill the evil stepmother, save her kingdom, and take her rightful place as heir to the throne. As in more traditional versions, in *Snow White and the Huntsman*, Snow White has a special relationship with animals, evidenced here by a rare sighting of a unicorn that allows her to approach him. Although Snow White doesn't hunt or kill any animals, like other hunting girls she does run through the forest, learning to fight and fend for herself.

Like the other girls who are more at home in the forest than they are among their peers, *Twilight*'s Bella Swan is at home among the vampires and their forest-stalking ways than she is among her high school classmates. In fact, when Bella marries Edward, her high school friends are absent from the films or the books, which focus

FIGURE 3.7 Bella (Kristen Stewart) kills a mountain lion in *Twilight: Breaking Dawn–Part 2* (2012), directed by Bill Condon.

on her new family of vampires and wolves. In the third install-ment, *Breaking Dawn–Part I*, when Jacob imprints on Bella's new-born daughter Renesmee, the wolves and vampires form a close alliance, so much so that they risk their lives for one another in the final film (and book). Bella lives among animals and animal-human hybrids. She ends up hunting mountain lions and deer with bloodthirsty lust.

In the book, much is made of the fact that she shreds her dress during her first hunt and Edward finds this very sexy. In fact, Bella's hunting seems to turn him on. And she finds it sensually exciting too: "My jaws locked easily over the precise point where the heat flow concentrated . . . my teeth were steel razors; they cut through the fur and fat and sinews like they weren't there . . . the blood was hot and wet and it soothed the ragged, itching thirst as I drank in an eager rush. The cat's struggles grew more and more feeble, and his screams choked off with a gurgle. The warmth of his blood radiated through my whole body, heating even my fingertips and toes" (Meyer 2008:422–23). The last installment of *The Twilight Saga* is filled with jokes about Bella's strength and the force of her appetites, both her sexual appetites and her thirst for blood. The transition from girlhood to womanhood, and human to vampire, has turned her into a voracious animal with limitless appetites.

Throughout *The Twilight Saga*, Bella has wanted Edward to change her into a vampire. She longs to leave behind her pubescent female body and exchange it for a stronger, bloodless body. Of course, blood is a central character in this vampire story. It is noteworthy, however, that the most blood we see is Bella's.[7] She bleeds in every episode, whether it is an accidental paper-cut that sets Edward's vampire siblings aflame or a purposeful ruse to lure evil vampires in the wrong direction. Perhaps the bloodiest moment in the series is the scene in which Bella gives birth to Renesmee, thanks to Edward's chewing through the amniotic sac with his teeth, after Edward's vampire sister Rosalee begins to perform a C-section with a scalpel but has to leave the room because the sight of Bella's blood is overpowering.[8] Bella's womanly blood is too much for the vampires, who are constantly challenged to control their urges to taste it. More importantly, Bella's womanly blood is too much for Bella herself who wants to overcome her awkward bleeding body by dying and becoming a vampire. She would rather be undead than a living breathing teenage girl who bleeds. Throughout the series, she comments on her clumsiness and awkwardness; and it is only in the last installment, after she is a vampire, that she says, "after eighteen years of being utterly ordinary, now is my chance to shine." *Twilight* is a coming-of-age fairytale wherein the girl overcomes her fears of puberty and menstruation by becoming a bloodless vampire.

In terms of the traditional role of the female lead and its endorsement of traditional romance and family values, *Twilight* is conservative—even if that family is an extended family of vampires. It is also closer to traditional fairytales than other recent

Young Adult literature and films in that Bella marries her prince (even if he is a prince of darkness) in what has been described as a fairytale wedding. Bella's is a familiar story of Beauty and the Beast. Even her name, *Bella,* means beautiful in Italian. But rather than Beauty's love transforming the beast into a handsome prince, the Beast transforms her into a beautiful, if also beastly, vampire. Bella becomes both beauty and the beast. In this updated version of Beauty and the Beast, the Beast is also already beautiful and Beauty wants nothing more than to become a beast. The union of beauty and beast, of human and animalesque creature, creates an everlasting bond, an eternal romance for a couple destined to be forever young and beautiful; and it creates a beautiful daughter, who we learn at the end of the film is also an immortal. Bella gives birth to an eternally beautiful fairytale family, born out of the blood and violence of the clash between human and vampire worlds, and the exclusion of hybrids and laws against miscegenation within the vampire code.[9] Her baby comes through violent sex that leaves her bruised and battered. As in many classic fairytales, her "happily ever after" is bought through violence, in this case her own as much as that of her prince. In *Fifty Shades of Grey*, Edward's porno alter ego Christian is the beast who is tamed through Anastasia's love. And again, their happiness is bought through sexual violence exercised by Christian on Ana. In *Twilight*, Bella is physically hurt and badly bruised during sex with Edward but, in classic pornutopia fashion, comes back for more.

DIVERGENT'S BEATRICE: AWAKING SLEEPING BEAUTY

While *Divergent*'s Beatrice "Tris" Prior (Shailene Woodley) doesn't hunt and kill animals, like her recent filmic sisters she is a tough sixteen-year-old girl who is both predator and prey. Although Tris says, "I am birdlike, made narrow and small as if for taking flight," she is more likely to fight than take flight. As the story goes, Beatrice Prior is born into the Abnegation faction and both the book and film open with her life there, a life of selflessness where unlimited access to mirrors is forbidden. Beatrice and her brother Caleb undergo aptitude testing wherein Beatrice finds out she is "Divergent," which means she has characteristics of various factions and could choose any of them, most especially Abnegation, Dauntless, and Erudite. When the leader of Erudite, the evil queen of the story, Jeanine (Kate Winslet), subjects Tris to a simulation wherein the last and most difficult for her to pass is Amity; to pass she must not only remain passive and not fight Jeanine but also quit fighting against herself to the point of self-forgiveness.

It is noteworthy that the theme of forgiveness and self-forgiveness appears in several of these recent films about tough girls. Tris is not the only one asking for, or giving, forgiveness. Maleficent asks forgiveness from her surrogate daughter Aurora, who gives it. *Frozen*'s Elsa asks forgiveness from her sister Anna, who gives it. And in Kenneth Branaugh's remake of *Cinderella* (2015), Ella (Lily James) forgives her evil stepmother (Cate Blanchett). Kindness and courage are explicit values repeated throughout *Cinderella*. Through her kindness, Ella forgives her stepmother and stepsisters, but through her courage she leaves her abusive home to return to the castle with the prince. Her recent filmic counterparts aren't so romantic and imperious in their forgiveness. In *Maleficent* and *Divergent* the protagonists face a violent world where they are violated body and soul, and where their attempts to meet violence with violence cause them as much trauma as their own victimization. Within the narrative of the films, like so many rape victims, these traumatized young women blame themselves and therefore must learn to forgive themselves.

Stepping outside of the narratives of the films, we could read their need for forgiveness as the need to be forgiven for being strong and courageous. And we could read their need for self-forgiveness as the need to forgive themselves for what they perceive as bringing violence on themselves. Tris is especially remorseful about how her violence caused the death of her friend. Furthermore, in the context of rape myths that blame the victim, the need to ask for forgiveness and to forgive themselves could be interpreted as the internalization of blame placed on them by rape culture. When she is given truth serum, Tris tearfully confesses that she is violent and that she is to blame. Only later, through a simulated encounter with her mother, does she learn to forgive herself. Tris is as traumatized by her own violence as she is by the violence of others around her. Ultimately, she is afraid of herself because she is aware of her own participation in the violence all around her. Her confession is the most angst-filled scene in *Insurgent* (the second film in the series) because she holds herself responsible for her own trauma. If she suffers from PTSD, she believes that she's brought it on herself. And forgiving herself for her own violence is the most difficult thing she has to do. Her greatest demon is her self-blame, and this becomes clear in the simulations in *Insurgent* when her last feat during a "sim" is forgiving herself.

A recurring theme in the *Divergent* books and films are simulations in which the subject must face his or her worst fears; how they do so determines which faction suits them. This means that Tris and other Divergents must hide their ability to pass tests in different factions. What Tris can do that most others can't is remain self-aware in the simulation and thereby distinguish reality from fantasy. Reminiscent of Katniss, who reassures Peeta when something is real or not real, seeing her reflection in pools of water or in glass represents Tris's self-awareness and her realization that "this is not real." These strong girls need to be able to distinguish between what is real and what is a simulation in order to survive. They can't be taken in by high-tech media illusion, which could be interpreted as symbols for social media, both its dangers and its liberating potential. Like *The Hunger Games*, *Divergent* plays with the tension between reality and fantasy by repeatedly drawing the audience into what seems to be real but turns out to be part of a simulation. As we have seen, the most powerful example is when we think that Four is congratulating Tris for passing a simulation, but instead he forces himself on her as part of the simulation. As discussed earlier, this rape-fantasy/fear is projected on the screen for all to see. Tris is a modern-day Sleeping Beauty who stays awake for fear of being raped.

Exposing deep fantasies and fears is a recurring theme throughout the *Divergent* series. Teens must publicly expose and face their deepest fears as they are tested in simulations. There is paranoia in this insistence on a culture that can see into your mind and even into your unconscious. In this high-tech and medicalized future, brainy scientists from the Erudite faction develop mind-control techniques that are irresistible for all but Divergents. The simulations that re-create their unconscious fears and project them onto big screens terrify even Divergents. These screens that display the inner workings of the mind for all to see, and that make the most intimate fears and desires public, can be read as a metaphor for social media. In this case, like *The Hunger Games*, *Divergent* is a warning against the dangers of invasive technologies like social media that let strangers, possibly even predators, into your private space. In addition, once again we see the theme of nature versus technology wherein technology is threatening. The Erudite faction develops technologies that are used to control the population. Their mind control is used to manipulate and deploy the Dauntless faction as mindless drones massacring the Abnegation faction. The Erudite want to prevent anyone from leaving the city or crossing the high-tech wall that separates the city from whatever is left of nature outside the wall. By the end of the story, however, Tris and Four escape the city with its technological evils and return to a more peaceful existence in nature. They also find temporary respite with the Amity faction on their farms where they tend the land and grow food. Here, the connections between nature and loving kindness, and between technology and intelligent evil, are explicit.

If Tris Prior is a princess, however, she is unlike any of those we have seen before. For one thing, unlike Katniss or Bella, once awakened from Abnegation into Dauntless, our contemporary

Sleeping Beauty is never shown wearing a ball gown or dancing with her prince. Rather, she goes from plain gray robes that cover her entire body to tight T-shirts and leather jackets that make her look tough and sexy but not like a princess. In the first film, she has a teenage Lara Croft look, with formfitting black leather pants and pushup bras. At the beginning of *Insurgent*, however, to mourn her parents and her friend Will, and seemingly as penance insofar as she blames herself for their deaths, she cuts off her hair. (Haircuts are another recurring theme. *Divergent* begins with Beatrice's mother trimming her long hair and offering her a momentary glance at herself in a mirror hidden in a cabinet.) Now, with her short haircut and boy's clothes, she looks more butch than princess. Her look has changed dramatically from the first film to the second as she trades in her tight leather for loose khakis and her pushup bra for boys' tank top undershirts. With her short hair and boys' clothes, she can easily pass for one of the boys—the princess becomes the prince.

In sum, as for Hanna, Katniss, and Bella before her, for Tris the transition from girlhood to womanhood is violent and threatening. These tough girls may be traumatized, but ultimately they find ways to cope. Certainly, with Hanna, Katniss, Bella, and Tris we have fairytale heroines who are tougher and more violent than their predecessors. They are no-nonsense girls-cum-women who prove their strength and prowess by hunting and killing animals. With these powerful girls the fairytale sustains itself. To quote the tagline from *Hanna*, "Adapt or Die." The fairytale and its princess adapt. If these films that feature hunting, hunted, and haunted girls are the latest adaptations of classic fairytales, then they undermine traditional ideals of femininity and romance even as they idealize our teenage heroines. Hanna discovers that the real world of real girls is not her world; and moreover, it is cruel and more painful than the forest where she grew up. Katniss discovers that both the Capitol and the rebels are corrupt and power-hungry. She settles for Peeta because she needs his calming presence. Unlike her idealistic princess predecessors, Katniss is a realist. She doesn't believe in the rhetoric coming from either side of the war. She doesn't pine for a prince. Rather, at the end of the book trilogy, playing a game they developed to get through the traumas of the war, when Peeta asks Katniss, "You love me. Real or not real?" she replies, "Real." These are two traumatized bruised souls confessing their love for each other, which is not the traditional flower petals and wedding-dress type of romance of classic fairytales.

Like Katniss and Peeta, Tris and Four are also traumatized and bond to overcome the violence of their world. And while Tris continually sacrifices herself for others, an Abnegation trait that is also a stereotypical feminine trait, she also takes what she wants. Like *The Hunger Games*, *Divergent* revolves around distinguishing fantasy from reality. And it is the girls who do this best. While others around them are taken in, they see through the illusions and take down the powers that be through their determination and guts. Both Tris and Katniss fall in love with traumatized boys and help them overcome their fears, help them heal their wounds, and thereby take up a traditional feminine role as nurse and care-giver; yet, attracted to trauma, trying to save the boy from his own demons, they also become more powerful. Both Katniss and Tris must awaken their boyfriends, who have been brainwashed by the evil powers that be. They become the keepers of reality. Katniss continually reassures Peeta about reality, and Tris continually sees through the illusions in simulations. Bella's is the only truly fairytale romance wherein the girl is swept off her feet (literally) by her prince. Even so, the forces of evil that threaten to keep them apart are more deadly and violent than ever. And Bella is the one who ends up protecting her prince and not the other way around.

The question remains, then, whether these equal-opportunity killers are new feminist role models or patriarchal fantasies of phallic girls with guns and arrows. I've argued that they are both. These hunting, hunted girls prove their strength in the traditional manly way by hunting and killing animals. As predators, they are strong and fearless. Yet in their pursuit of animals, they are portrayed as closer to animals, even identified with them. In spite of their new roles as hunters and predators, then, these girls continue to occupy the more traditional role as prey. Furthermore, girl power and feminine empowerment are reduced to violently fighting back, and killing innocent animals. For our contemporary princesses, there are few options for success and survival other than becoming as strong and as violent as the adult men around them. Their transformation from nature to technology, from girl to woman, is always accompanied by violence met with violence. In this generation of fairytales, these hunting, hunted, haunted girls take care of themselves. Katniss and Tris do so through their uncanny ability to distinguish fantasy from reality. Hanna does so by fighting any man who comes her way. These girls on the cusp of womanhood represent the lost innocence of girlhood/nature now threatened by the corrupting, violent, even cruel influence of high-tech culture, symbolized by the screen: in Hanna, her first encounter with a television screen is terrifying; Katniss is tormented by her own image on the deadly reality television show called the "Hunger Games"; and Tris's most intimate and secret fears and desires are projected onto giant computer screens for all to see. Their sexual transformation from girls to women is paralleled by the transition from innocent nature to threatening technological culture, from innocent girlhood to the dangers of womanhood. In a violent world where assault is the norm, these girls give as good as they get, but they get plenty. They learn to survive by recognizing that their reflections in media and on screens are not real. These princesses no longer believe in fairytales as an escape from the violence of reality all around them. Rather, they are subjected to violence and assault, even from the princes who love them. No longer content with the Disney fantasy of princesses who want to be awakened by a kiss from a prince, these tough hunting girls sleep with one eye open just waiting to fight off an attack from their boyfriends or anyone else.

CONCLUSION

THE NEW ARTEMIS, TITLE IX, AND TAKING RESPONSIBILITY FOR SEXUAL ASSAULT

IN THE CONTEXT OF ANALYZING images of tough girls competing with boys in Young Adult literature and film, it is fascinating that Title IX legislation, associated primarily with equal opportunities for girls in high school and college athletics, has become a turning point in discussions of sexual assault. Until recently, the greatest impact of the 1972 Title IX legislation had been to ensure girls and women access to sports.[1] Although introduced to stop discrimination in higher education, Title IX became the hallmark of women's athletics, to the point that today there is a women's sporting clothing company named Title Nine, and in 2015 President Obama spoke about the importance of Title IX for girls in terms of his own experience coaching his girls' basketball team and the confidence it gave the girls. Initially, Title IX was used to secure funding for girls and women's sports, which had been lacking until required by this federal statute.

Recent Young Adult literature and films that feature tough girls successfully competing with boys in sports such as archery, boxing, weight lifting, rope climbing, shooting, and various forms of fighting are Title IX dreams come true. Katniss Everdeen's preparations for the Hunger Games, and Tris Prior's training to join the Dauntless faction, are fantasies not only of gender equality in sports but also of girls competing with boys and winning. These girls beat boys at their own games. Films like *Hanna*, *The Hunger Games*, and *Divergent* are images of Title IX in action. In these contemporary fairytales, girls must learn to compete with boys in order to survive. The new Artemis, goddess of the hunt, refuses to be any man's prey. She is fighting off sexual assault, if not to protect her virginity, then to call the shots sexually. The new Artemis figures in film may be traumatized and abused, but ultimately, physically, they get the upper hand. The hunted become the huntress.

In Greek mythology, Artemis is a virgin goddess, who, born first, helps her mother with the birth of her twin brother, Apollo. On her birthday, she asks her father for eternal virginity, a bow and arrows, a tunic and hunting clothes, along with virgin nymphs as hunting companions. With her wishes granted, Artemis is often portrayed in a boy's tunic with a bow and arrows, accompanied by nymphs. She is goddess of the hunt, lives in the forest, and both hunts and protects animals. She ruthlessly defends her virginity against any challenges to it, and fights off several attempted rapes throughout her life. Many times, along with Apollo, she defends her mother, Leto, who seems incapable of defending herself. Like Hanna, Katniss, and Bella, Artemis is associated with nature and wild animals. Although she is an expert archer not afraid to use her arrows against any who threaten her, she is also depicted as compassionate and healing, especially toward girls and young animals. Never marrying, she is one of the most independent and self-sufficient of the goddesses, with a soft spot for mothers and their young. Like Artemis, the girl hunters in recent film—Hanna, Katniss, and Merida—are virgins, who use bows and arrows to defend or protect their mothers and their own honor.

Artemis has become the symbol of strong girls and women in film—as evidenced by the proliferation of images of hunting girls, along with the fact that a film production company called Artemis Films sponsors the Artemis Film Festival, which celebrates powerful "females on film who are fearless, fierce, and revolutionary" and "women who kick ass."[2] Our teen heroines definitely kick ass. Hanna, Bella, Katniss, and Tris, along with their younger sisters Hit Girl, Merida, and some of Disney's latest princesses, give as good as they get. In spite of, or because of, the fact that they are bruised and battered in the process, these girls also band together with other girls and women—friends, sisters, and mothers—to form unbreakable bonds to support each other through their traumatic encounters; these girls and women work together to resist the oppressive authority of corrupt officials. Hanna befriends teenager Sophie; Bella has her vampire sisters-in-law; Katniss volunteers for the Hunger Games to save her beloved sister Primrose and befriends young Rue during the games; Tris relies on her Dauntless girlfriends and a strong bond with her mother; even *Brave*'s young Merida protects her mother, and in the end they ride off into the sunset together; in *Frozen* it is love between sisters Anna and Elsa that breaks the evil curse; and in *Maleficent* true love's kiss is given by a mother surrogate to young Aurora. In addition to their ability to fight like boys and compete in a man's world, these girls bond together and love and protect each other.

Like Artemis who, in Greek mythology, saves infant Atalanta from exposure after her father had left her to die because she was female, our new Artemis figures take care of their sisters. Like Artemis, who mentors Atalanta to be a strong goddess athlete holding her own against boys and men in foot races, wrestling matches, and hunting, our hunting girls in film take care of their younger sisters. Artemis also teaches Atalanta to defend herself against the threat of sexual assault, which, as we know from all those stories of raping gods and victimized goddesses, was the stuff of legends on Mount Olympus. Atalanta and Artemis defend each other; they've got each other's backs. They support each other through their sporting competitions with men. More importantly, they defend each other from sexual assault. These virgin goddesses can defend themselves and each other independently of men. They don't need to be rescued by a prince or a god.

The two facets of the Artemis/Atalanta myths—competitive sports and defense against rape—resonate with the evolving history of Title IX, first to address inequities in college athletics and now to address an atmosphere that ignores or even encourages sexual assault. The strong independent goddesses can hold their own against men. Their bond empowers them in their struggles for freedom from sexual assault. Their survival is dependent upon their bonding together. Without Artemis, Atalanta wouldn't have lived.

Responding to the so-called "Atalanta complex," which leaves girls exposed to devaluation and degradation just as Atalanta was exposed to the elements and left to die, in the context of discussing the importance of Title IX to women's sports, Margaret Carlisle Duncan writes, "Girls develop into resourceful, self-reliant women by being supported and encouraged in their endeavors. They develop with the help of mentors and role models. And they develop by virtue of social structures that are built to enable rather than disable the growth of female self-worth. Perhaps we can think of Artemis as symbolically fulfilling these conditions" (Duncan 2006).[3] Duncan proposes that Artemis figures are advocates of girls who take up their cause and defend their Title IX rights to education and an empowered sense of self. "The promise of Artemis," she says, "is the empowerment of girls" (Duncan 2006). In addition to being the goddess of the hunt, Artemis has become a symbol of Title IX and its success in bringing more women into sports, and also of women and girls helping and mentoring each other (Duncan 2006; Samuels 2011:34). Our new Artemis figures in film fit the bill. They are goddesses of the hunt and bond together with their sisters to defend and protect themselves and those they love.

In addition, then, to critically focusing on the violence of girls toward animals and each other, and rather than extol the ways in which tough girls on screen have become equal-opportunity killers, we can embrace the ways in which these strong role models for young girls bond together with their sisters to stand up against violence toward them. While they may fight violence with more violence, they successfully ward off the worst violence in order to survive. They are fighting for their mothers (Merida, Katniss, Tris, Hanna), daughters (Bella, Maleficent), sisters (Katniss), and friends (Hanna, Tris). Whatever else they are, they are survivors. And rather than just focus on their violence, we should emphasize the ways in which girl power in these films is also the result of girls and women bonding together to nurture and protect each other.

The promise of the new Artemis is the empowerment of girls and women, and their greatest strengths are not just their hunting prowess and equal-opportunity killings, but rather their mentoring and support of the other girls and women in their lives. By these criteria, the true Artemises on film may not be Hanna, Bella, Katniss, or Tris, but rather the heroines of the anti-rape documentary *The Hunting Ground*—survivors Annie Clark and Andrea Pino, cofounders of EROC (End Rape on Campus), and survivor Emma Sulkowicz a.k.a. "Mattress Girl," and many others on college campuses around the country who are fighting against sexual violence, not with violence of their own but rather with social media, compassionate activism, and performance art. These real-life heroines are not afraid to tell their stories, even if it means facing retaliation and death threats in order to bring sexual violence out of the shadows and into the spotlight. Much of the recent attention to sexual assault as a Title IX violation is the result of a lawsuit filed against the University of North Carolina by Annie Clark and Andrea Pino, two undergraduates raped during their first weeks on campus. Both Annie Clark and Andrea Pino reported the attacks to the university, but they claim their reports were ignored or belittled. These two courageous women have made headlines for their anti-rape activism. And their use of Title IX has changed the terms of discussions over sexual assault on campus. Even those who insist that "rapists cause rape" have to rethink the strategy of isolating perpetrators from the culture that produces them.

In a society that values individual responsibility over institutional responsibility, it is interesting that educational institutions are being held responsible for sexual violence. In large part, thanks to the efforts of anti-rape activists Annie Clark and Andrea Pino, survivors across the country are filing Title IX lawsuits against their colleges and universities for allowing serial rapists to remain on campus, making the environment unsafe for female students. This strategy targets the educational institutions that harbor rapists rather than the rapists themselves. It holds schools responsible for sexual assault on campus. Rather than excuse the problem with the argument that a few bad apples spoil the whole bunch, this approach looks to systematic policies of disavowal and denial, of lack of attention to the problem, and lack of consequences for perpetrators, rather than just targeting individuals. Whether or not this approach will be successful remains to be seen. Still, it signals a major shift in the way we view responsibility, moving from individual responsibility that blames individual psychology, pathology, or criminality, to institutional responsibility that blames a whole culture, or at least a subset of it. If rape myths blame victims, and activists respond by insisting perpetrators be held responsible, the Title IX strategy shifts the blame from either set of individuals to the institutions that shelter sexual assault. In this regard, anti-rape activism is on the vanguard of shifting blame and responsibility from individuals to social systems and institutions. If ours is a rape culture, then the solution must also address the culture of sexual violence that perpetuates sexual assault.

The irony is that while anti-rape activists and survivors of sexual assault are using Title IX to force colleges and universities to address the problem of sexual violence on campus, Title IX is also being used to shut down discussions of sexual violence on campus, possibly the very kinds of discussions necessary to combat rape myths. For example, when a student group at Brown University organized a debate about whether or not we live in a "rape culture," and whether or not culture is to blame for rape, a member of another student group, the Sexual Assault Task Force, protested on the grounds that the debate might "trigger" trauma in survivors. To provide a "safe space" for those who might feel troubled or "triggered," members of Sexual Assault Task Force set up a room with cookies, coloring books, bubbles, a video of puppies, and Play-Doh, where those triggered could go to recover and feel "safe." One student, a "rape survivor and 'sexual assault peer educator' who helped set up the room and worked in it during the debate, estimates that a couple of dozen people used it. At one point she went to the lecture hall—it was packed—but after a while, she had to return to the safe space. 'I was feeling bombarded by a lot of viewpoints that really go against my dearly and closely held beliefs'" (Shulevitz 2015).

Triggers and trigger warnings take the hunting metaphor into the classroom and onto college campuses in a way that threatens to shut down rather than open up the possibility of addressing sexual violence. The use of the word "trigger" suggests a weapon, a gun, or even a bow that has a trigger. Words are seen as weapons that can wound and traumatize. The student who felt "bombarded" during the discussion of rape culture at Brown University felt under attack by viewpoints she didn't share. And yet traditionally colleges and universities are places where "dearly and closely held beliefs" are supposed to be critically examined. Often educators say that their goal is to encourage critical thinking in the classroom. Avoiding triggering material undermines this goal, especially in terms of the most pressing social issues facing students today. If we cannot critically analyze rape culture, then how can we begin to address the problem of rape myths and their role in sexual assault? If trigger warnings are required before discussing anything that might trigger someone's individual trauma, whatever it might be, then every syllabus and every class in the humanities may need to contain trigger warnings, especially if the goal of education is critical thinking about our most cherished beliefs, desires, and fears. Obviously, educators need to be sensitive to students and their experiences; and this may require finding ways to present difficult material to encourage critical discussions without further injuring students who have been the victims of sexual violence.

It is telling that the upsurge of the call for trigger warnings is a response to discussions of sexual violence on campus. A statement by the American Association of University Professors on trigger warnings concludes: "It is probably not coincidental that the call for trigger warnings comes at a time of increased attention to campus violence, especially to sexual assault that is often associated with the widespread abuse of alcohol. Trigger warnings are a way of displacing the problem, however, locating its solution in the classroom rather than in administrative attention to social behaviors that permit sexual violence to take place. Trigger warnings will not solve this problem, but only misdirect attention from it and, in the process, threaten the academic freedom of teachers and students whose classrooms should be open to difficult discussions, whatever form they take" (AAUP 2014). Trigger warnings also displace the problem of sexual assault onto discussions of sexual assault. The problem seemingly becomes talking about sexual assault rather than sexual assault itself. Furthermore, talking about sexual assault in critical ways that may help combat rape myths reportedly becomes another form of assault. Conversations about rape culture apparently are akin to photography of rape posted on the Internet, in that they retraumatize and continue the harm of assault into an indefinite future that prevents victims from healing. Nonetheless, conversations about rape culture are necessary in order to begin to address the ways in which various institutions from fairytales to fraternities promote sexual assault and the rape of unconscious girls.

Again, it is telling that the call for trigger warnings began in the blogosphere to signal graphic descriptions of rape on feminist sites. Survivors claimed that they might be triggered by reading about another victim's rape. The idea is that PTSD is triggered by words or images that cause flashbacks, and before someone pulls that trigger, they should give warning. Most of the people asking for trigger warnings feel they have been traumatized or abused by sexism or racism or assault in ways that make them sensitive and easily triggered. We live in a culture of wounded, traumatized subjects, reminiscent of the Young Adult dystopias presented in recent literature and films. Yet the kind of censorship suggested by trigger warnings, and calls for colleges and universities to avoid subjects that might trigger PTSD or trauma in victims or survivors, can be used to discourage women from speaking out about their experiences and making others aware of the problem of sexual violence. The danger is that students cannot distinguish between critical discussions of sexual violence and forms of sexual violence. The insistence on trigger warnings and safe spaces full of cookies and pictures of puppies could work to further infantilize and pathologize victims, even as it raises awareness of the trauma of sexual assault for victims.

At the same time that Title IX is being used to fight against sexual violence on campus, it is being wielded to stop debates about sexual violence or other forms of social injustice that might offend some students. Students expect campuses to be safe places, not only physically safe but also emotionally safe. Title IX is being used to pressure universities to take responsibility for sexual assault on campus, and it is being used to pressure them to stop any discussions of sexual assault that may trigger survivors. As Judith Shulevitz points out, "Universities are in a double bind. They're required by two civil-rights statutes, Title VII and Title IX, to ensure that their campuses don't create a 'hostile environment' for women and other groups subject to harassment. However, universities are not supposed to go too far in suppressing free speech, either. If a university cancels a talk or punishes a professor and a lawsuit ensues, history suggests that the university will lose. But if officials don't censure or don't prevent speech that may inflict psychological damage on a member of a protected class, they risk fostering a hostile environment and prompting an investigation. As a result, students who say they feel unsafe are more likely to be heard than students who demand censorship on other grounds" (2015). One telling example is the student protest at Smith College against "free-speech advocate Wendy Kaminer, who had been arguing against the use of the euphemism 'the n-word' when teaching American history or 'The Adventures of Huckleberry Finn.'" Kaminer responded, "It's amazing to me that they can't distinguish between racist speech and speech about racist speech, between racism and discussions of racism" (Shulevitz 2015). In an attempt to be politically correct, some students are aiming Title IX at the very faculty advocates who are committed to overcoming social injustice.

While the federal government is demanding more accountability from colleges and universities around the issue of sexual violence, some students are protesting when faculty speak out in ways they deem insensitive to their trauma and suffering. For example, recently at Northwestern University students protested against a faculty member, Laura Kipnis, who wrote an essay about relationships between students and faculty in the age of what she called "sexual paranoia," which students claimed discounted charges by two students that a philosophy professor had sexually assaulted them. Students protested the essay by carrying mattresses and bringing a Title IX suit against the author of the essay and the university, claiming that the essay was making the university a hostile place for rape victims.[4] Echoing Emma Sulkowicz's performance piece "Carry That Weight," students used the symbol of sexual assault, the mattress, against a professor who wrote an essay that jokingly defended sexual freedom and jokingly disparaged sexual harassment. The author called into question the designation "survivor," a term taken from Holocaust survivors, for people she said should be called "accusers," since no sexual assault had been proven. While Kipnis unnecessarily makes light of sexual harassment and survivors, she does bring up the critical question of what we mean by "survivor" and what it is that discussing sensitive subjects "triggers." The mattress protests against her seem to prove her point in that they conflate talking about sexual harassment with perpetrating it. For all its problems, and there are many, Kipnis's essay is not just an apology for sexual harassment but also raises important questions in debates over trauma culture and the ability of trigger warnings and Title IX investigations to close down rather than open up discussion. What the Kipnis case demonstrates is the murky territory of Title IX, which is almost as confusing and confused as the issue of consent in the age of intoxication. The Kipnis affair raises the question, Who is responsible for creating a safe environment for education and how can we go about it in an era of increased awareness to sexual violence that sometimes leads to "trigger-happy" students and others shutting down discussions because they are too painful to have?

Those who have lived their entire lives in a post-9/11 world may have grown up with the notion that everyone is traumatized and we are all survivors. Certainly, the rhetoric of *trauma, survivor*, and *PTSD* has proliferated to the point that seemingly anyone could have PTSD for just about anything; and everyone could be susceptible to triggers setting off their trauma. Feeling unsafe or feeling hurt have become grounds for claiming the position of victim. There is an increasing attention to affect in both academic circles and in culture more generally. But while within scholarly research there is critical analysis of affects, within popular culture there is often an embrace of sentimentality that uncritically views emotions and affects as subjective truths that exist in a vacuum and that cannot be questioned. In the context of Homeland Security, and the national obsession with safety and security from unseen attackers and terrorist threats that could come from any place, safety has become the ultimate value. Yet within the popular discourse of trauma, increasingly safety includes emotional safe spaces where young people won't get their feeling hurt by hearing what they don't want to hear.

Title IX has gone from addressing funding and quantifiable differences between resources spent on men's and women's athletics and educational programs, to addressing the ethos of educational institutions in terms of whether or not they foster or empower girls and women. Title IX has gone from addressing formal equality in education to addressing social justice. While this is a step forward, it must be taken in the context of critical analysis of the politics of affect and the role of the social in social justice. Once we take the

first step in moving from liberal individualism in terms of responsibility to social responsibility for rape and sexual assault, then, as
we have seen, we must consider not only the ways in which consent
continues to be limited by the framework of liberal individualism
and limited notions of sexual autonomy, but also how consent is
socially governed, if not determined, by the norms and values of
dominant culture. In other words, we have to open up rather than
close down discussions of rape culture and the contributions of
rape myths, sexism, and hostility toward women, to the prevalence
of sexual violence.

In a culture that increasingly values feelings and legitimates sensitivity to triggers and traumas caused by words rather than by deeds
and embraces the power of language to injure, the equal legitimation
of all feelings becomes a form of political leveling. Feelings reduced to
mere sentiments uncritically held as true moves us dangerously close
to a form of reactionary politics that closes down discussions that
are too difficult, on the one hand, and cannot distinguish between
sexism or racism and critical discussions of them, on the other.
As the sentiment of the student who took refuge in the safe space of
the cookie room at Brown during the discussion of rape suggests,
the demand for trigger warnings and safe spaces is a demand for
agreement of feelings where agreement is defined as agreeing with
the individual claiming to be triggered. In a culture where the positions of *victim* and *survivor* have become valorized, where victims
are the norm instead of the exception, students demand emotional
safety from feelings they don't like. As Lauren Berlant so powerfully
argues, the "minority subject" position of victimization has become
desirable, and political discourse has been thereby reduced to feelings rather than critical analysis (Berlant 1994:154).

As a result of the valorization of the position of victim, and in
the name of the undeniable truth of subjective feelings, perpetrators of sexual violence can claim to be victims, and survivors of
sexual assault can close down discussions that might help prevent
assault in the future. On the one hand, the perpetrators of sexual
assault can take up the position of victim by claiming defamation

and that their careers have been ruined. On the other hand, survivors demand safe spaces where they don't have to hear about sexual violence for fear of triggering their PTSD. The risk, then, is that educating about sexual violence will itself become a "trigger" for past trauma, and students will insist that they want to be safe not only from sexual assault but also from any talk of sexual assault. This makes Title IX a double-edged tool in addressing sexual violence on campus. Universities are being held responsible to safeguard the feelings of all of their students; these students could at any time claim the status of victim, whether as a victim of sexual assault, or as a victim of a smear campaign for committing sexual assault, or a just victim of hurt feelings.

In light of the emphasis on feelings in contemporary culture, it is interesting that the word *consent* is from the Latin *con* (together, with) and *sentire* (feel). *Consent* means an agreement of feelings. This agreement of feelings has come to mean an agreement to do something, or more precisely, to allow something to be done to you. In terms of affirmative consent to sex, it has been interpreted as a contract of sorts, framed by classical notions of individual autonomy, which as we have seen is problematic. Yet, in Latin, *sentire* can mean not only feelings as in emotion or belief but also sensing as in perception or knowledge. Additionally, the root of *sentire*, *sentio*, means to go, or to head for, as in a path, a way, or a journey, which in some languages such as German and Lithuanian is associated with thinking. Consent, then, means being sensitive to each other, sensing and perceiving the agreement of the other. Furthermore, consent could be reinterpreted as a journey together, with thinking as much as with feeling. Obviously, the journey of consent cannot begin with one party passed out or semiconscious while the other party disregards her feelings. Both *affirmative consent* and *nonconsensual sex* as they are presently used within discussions of party rape on campus undermine the notion of consent as a thoughtful journey together.

As we have seen, rape myths and the ethos of rape culture on college campuses valorizes a lack of consent. Recently, the federal government endorsed the use of Title IX to hold colleges and universities responsible for this ethos that encourages party rape and sexual assault. On April 4, 2011, the United States Department of Education sent a "Dear Colleague Letter" to institutions of higher learning reminding them that Title IX prohibits discrimination on the basis of sex, which includes sexual violence and rape. The letter goes on to define sexual violence as "physical sexual acts perpetrated against a person's will or where a person is incapable of giving consent due to the victim's use of drugs or alcohol," including "sexual assault, sexual battery, and sexual coercion" (2011). The letter explains that schools have a "responsibility to take immediate and effective steps to end sexual harassment and sexual violence" (2011). The responsibility for stopping sexual assault is being placed on educational institutions, which are expected not only to appropriately and swiftly respond to instances of alleged sexual assault but also to prevent sexual violence on campus. Several studies indicate that education can help prevent sexual assault through eradicating rape myths, most especially the pornutopian idea that women enjoy rape (Hamilton & Yee 1990; Mohler-Kuo et al. 2004; Armstrong et al. 2006; Burnett et al. 2009; Krebs et al. 2009; Jozkowski & Peterson 2014).

If, as my analysis in *Hunting Girls* suggests, images of girls beaten, bruised, and sexually assaulted form significant parts of mainstream entertainment, both in Hollywood films and on social media, then perhaps education is the right place to start, provided education can counteract the effects of rape myths perpetuated through the entertainment industry, especially pornography. After all, education has changed the way we have sex. For example "safe sex" campaigns made condom use the norm (Yzer 1999; McEnrue & Owens 2014). Some prison activists may see moving rape from a felony crime requiring incarceration into the realm of an honor code or Title IX civil rights violation as a step forward in rehabilitation.[5] Currently, however, educational institutions are not equipped to be rehabilitation centers for sex offenders. Moreover, colleges are in the business of education and not of punishment, which is why the Association for Student Conduct Administration has advised the use of education rather than punishment when handling campus rape (Kingkade 2014a). It remains to be seen how pending Title IX investigations affect school programs designed to address sexual violence and treat sex offenders. Currently, the harshest penalty a college or university can exact is expulsion, which leaves the perpetrator free to matriculate elsewhere. While it may be possible to sue for damages using Title IX, usually schools are the ones fined, not sex offenders (although there have been cases where colleges and universities levied minimal fines against offenders).

If educational institutions are to address the problem of sexual assault on campus, then they can't shy away from difficult discussions. Students need to be aware that crucially discussing sexual violence is not in itself a form of sexual violence, but rather is necessary as a first step to stopping it. One such difficult discussion is the role of alcohol and drugs in party rape. No one wants to be told that they can't party while in college. But if, as anti-rape activist and survivor Ari Mostov hopes, eventually "don't drink and assault someone" could become as ubiquitous as "don't drink and drive," then we need awareness campaigns that include education about the trauma to victims caused by sexual assault, and discussion of affirmative consent or that "only yes means yes." Just as "don't drink and drive" is backed up by the legal system that makes it illegal to drink and drive, sexual assault policies on campus need to be backed up by the legal system. We need coordinated efforts and policies between educational institutions and the legal system. If "only yes means yes" is to become the standard, then schools and government need to work together to change attitudes that contribute to sexual assault and to the lack of consequences to perpetrators of sexual violence.

Certainly, any number of other institutions—for example, sports, military, film, pornography, and advertising—contribute to the normalization of violence, including sexual violence, toward girls and women. Many of these other institutions, especially pornography, contribute to rape myths. Still, it may be appropriate to focus on colleges and universities because institutions such as sports and fraternities, which are especially prone to propagate rape myths and the denigration of women, are housed on or near campuses. In addition, rape rates are higher on college campuses than in the general population. In spite of this, many colleges and universities deny there is a problem. Obviously, in terms of attracting students and appeasing parents, they want to present their campuses as safe spaces. If passed, however, the Campus Accountability and Safety Act would make schools responsible for accurate reporting of sexual assaults. In addition to those that are officially reported, the law would require surveys to try to determine the actual rate of sexual assault on campus.[6] Already, the Clery Act, named for Jeanne Clery, a nineteen-year-old Lehigh University student who was raped and murdered by another student in her dorm room, requires schools to report all crimes and make those statistics public. Schools that don't adequately respond to reports of sexual violence can be subject to Title IX restrictions that withdraw federal funding—although it is important to note that so far this has never happened as a result of a Title IX violation, which suggests that Title IX may need more teeth to be effective in addressing the problem of sexual assault on campus.

Even in view of the "Dear Colleague Letter," and the media's spotlight on the "epidemic" of rape on campus, most college presidents deny there is a problem. "More than 100 institutions of higher learning are currently under federal investigation for potentially mishandling sexual assault complaints, but nearly 80 percent of college and university presidents say sexual assault isn't prevalent on their campuses . . . only 8 percent strongly agreed with the statement, 'sexual assault is prevalent at U.S. colleges and universities'" (Filipovic 2015). The near weekly reports in mainstream media of sexual misconduct, compounded by little or inappropriate responses from college administrators, makes clear that for the most part colleges try to cover up the problem rather than address it. They have a vested interest in maintaining their reputations as safe places for parents to send their children. In spite of overwhelming evidence that sexual assault is a problem on campuses across the country, over 40 percent of colleges and universities report no sexual assaults. If colleges have become "hunting grounds" for sexual predators who prey on young women, and if they are effectively safe havens for serial rapists who face little to no consequences for their sexual violence, then it seems reasonable to hold colleges and universities responsible for allowing rape to continue unchecked, even if schools are not themselves to blame for rape. The first step in addressing the rape "epidemic" on campus, however, is for colleges and universities to acknowledge the problem. Party rape and nonconsensual sex are rampant on college campuses, and educational institutions have a responsibility to address the ethos that contributes to sexual assault. Even if that ethos is spawned in the culture at large, it undermines not only the possibility of formal equality in education but also any hope of social justice, which demands more than equal-opportunity violence. In addition to the issue of individual sexual autonomy and subjective feelings, discussions of consent, affirmative consent, and nonconsensual sex need to address the social context of consent in the culture of rape from Sleeping Beauty to party rape on campus.

As we have seen, an alternative to seeing consent in terms of contracts or giving permission, we might view *consent* in terms of its more originary meaning, feeling with, or journey with. If consent is seen as a journey taken together rather than a legalistic protection to be gotten or given, then in a sense, we not only emphasize the intersubjectivity of feelings, and the possibility of sex as a form of communication but also mutual respect for, and sensitivity to, the response from the other.

An ethics of response, or what I have called *witnessing*, would promote versions of consent that open up rather than close down the possibility of conversation and critical thinking about our deepest desires and fears. *Witnessing* has the double sense of both eyewitness testimony, on the one hand, and witnessing to something beyond recognition on the other. The Latin *sentire* resonates with this tension at the heart of the concept of witnessing insofar as there are two dimensions of sense: *sense* as sensation, perception, or feeling, on the one hand, and *sense* as meaning, thinking, or knowing, on the other. Sense is both sensation and meaning, recognizable and beyond recognition. Witnessing as eyewitness testimony, however, cannot be reduced to subjective feelings but, as I describe it elsewhere, takes into account historical and social circumstances (Oliver 2001, 2004, 2015). Thinking of consent in terms of the double meaning of *sentire* highlights the tension between what we sense or perceive and what we take it to mean. Our experience is composed of both elements. And both are possible by virtue of a social and historical context. We see and mean by virtue of our culture, our language, and our traditions. Sexual assault does not happen in a vacuum. Rather, it happens in a culture whose primal fantasies and fairytales include the rape of unconscious girls and hallucinations of consent, and whose contemporary fantasies often are formed by pornography filled with images of violence toward girls and women, and Young Adult entertainment that revolves around images of beaten and battered girls.

In terms of response ethics, taking responsibility for sexual assault would entail considering the ways in which our culture encourages the denigration and assault of girls and women, from fairytales, to Hollywood blockbusters, to party rape on campus. Within a response ethics framework, consent would refer to a relationship, or thoughtful journey together, toward an agreement of feeling that opens up rather than closes off the possibility of response from another. This agreement of feelings could not shy away from difficult subjects, but rather would vigilantly pursue critical analysis of deep-seated fears and desires in order to get at the roots of what drives rape culture and the valorization and eroticization of nonconsensual sex with unconscious girls. Certainly, "no means no" and "only yes means yes," but, as we have seen, there is more to consider when addressing sexual assault on campus. In addition to holding individuals responsible, we have to consider the cultural ethos that makes rape possible, even desirable, an ethos in which lack of consent is valorized, and girls and women are viewed as prey or trophies to be hunted and vanquished. We need to continue to question a culture in which equal-opportunity killings of animals and each other by tough hunting girls is seen as entertainment, at best, or what it takes to address sexual inequality and social justice, at worst. We need to continue to examine new Artemis figures, both as role models for girls and women bonding together to fight social injustice, and as compensatory or revenge fantasies to counterbalance the real-world inequalities between men and women or boys and girls, and the social injustice that feeds them.

NOTES

INTRODUCTION: GIRLS AS TROPHIES

1. A recent study concludes: "Sexual violence on campus has reached epidemic levels: during their first year in college, one in seven women will have experienced incapacitated assault or rape and nearly one in 10 will have experienced forcible assault or rape" (Carey et. al. 2015).

2. See Bourke 2007; and Heyes 2016.

3. See Heyes 2016.

4. It is important to note that women are only vulnerable in this situation *because* men see it as an opportunity for sex.

5. See also Sanday 2007.

6. See also Bleecker & Murnan 2005; Sanday 2007.

7. It is important to note that men also rape other men. For discussions of man-on-man rape, see Sivakumaran 2005; Davies & Rogers 2006; White & Yamawaki 2009. These studies discuss the perception and stigma of homosexuality as silencing male victims. For a discussion of the different perceptions of female and male victims of rape, see Anderson 2007. For a discussion of rape of transgender people, see Stotzer 2009.

8. Cf. Kang 2012.

9. For a feminist analysis of the rise of women hunters, see Fitzgerald (2005). There, she criticizes what she sees as the liberal feminist notion that women hunting puts them on par with men and empowers women (2005:102).

10. Emily Gaarder says, "men may be attracted to hunting because of their need to provide for the family and show masculine prowess, and women may be

attached to animals due to maternal instincts" (Gaarder 2011:58–59). Feminists such as Emily Gaarder and Carol Adams have argued that in American culture, "real men" eat meat, while it is more acceptable for women to be vegetarians and animal activists, which is why far more women than men are vegetarians or animal activists (see Gaarder 2011). Adams shows connections between meat eating and our ideas about masculinity (1990, 2003): "Boy food doesn't grow. It is hunted or killed" (Adams 2003:92).

11. A report from the United States Department of Education concludes: "Acts of sexual violence are vastly under-reported. Yet, data show that our nation's young students suffer from acts of sexual violence early and the likelihood that they will be assaulted by the time they graduate is significant. For example: Recent data shows nearly 4,000 reported incidents of sexual battery and over 800 reported rapes and attempted rapes occurring *in our nation's public high schools.* Indeed, by the time girls graduate from high school, more than one in ten will have been physically forced to have sexual intercourse in or out of school. When young women get to *college*, nearly 20% of them will be victims of attempted or actual sexual assault, as will about 6% of undergraduate men" (2011).

1. A PRINCESS IS BEING BEATEN AND RAPED

1. See Projansky 2001a.

2. See Scott and Dargis 2011.

3. For a discussion of rape in U.S. cinema from 1903 to 1972, see Sarah Projanksy (2001a and 2001b). Projansky argues that rape is a central theme in Hollywood film (ibid.). She demonstrates how rape performs different functions in different genres. For example, she claims that in screwball comedies, rape is a response to tensions around women's independence and gender roles, while in westerns, rape functions to naturalize colonial conflict and racialization (2001a:82). See also Higgins and Silver, eds., *Rape and Representation* (1991). In her feminist classic, Susan Brownmiller discusses the "glamorization of rape" in popular film and culture (1975:302). For discussions of the difficulties of puberty for girls, especially in relationship to the threat of sexual violence, see Natsuaki et al. 2011; Reynolds & Juvonen 2011; Reynolds & Juvonen 2012. For a more phenomenological account, see Simone de Beauvoir's analysis of girlhood in *The Second Sex* (1949).

4. For insightful discussions of hookup culture, see Wolfe 2000, Bogle 2008, and Freitas 2013. For discussions of rape culture, see Buchwald et al. 2005.

5. Using a pseudonym, Anne Rice has written an erotic trilogy wherein Sleeping Beauty is a sex slave who eventually gains her freedom.

6. For a discussion of the medieval belief that women have to enjoy sex and have an orgasm to conceive, see Thomas Laqueur (1992).

7. In light of my analysis, it is noteworthy that within *Divergent* birds represent both a threat (the attacking crows), and family (represented by the three ravens Tris has tattooed on her shoulder to commemorate her past).

8. See YouTube "Divergent: Tris' Fear Simulation Test," posted on July 23, 2014, and comments afterwards.

9. For more analysis of the connection between sex and death in *Twilight*, see Oliver 2012.

10. For a discussion of ambiguity and ambivalence in *The Hunger Games* and other recent films, see Oliver 2014.

11. See Green 2015.

12. Cf. Orr 2015.

13. See Barker 2013, Dymock 2013, Martin 2013.

14. In 2007, the Justice Department estimated that one in ten college women were raped. But perhaps only 5 percent of victims report their rapes. The study also found that 90 percent of campus rapes are committed by as few as 4 percent of the men on campus (Rubenfeld 2014).

15. Cf. Warshaw 1994:104–110.

16. For a discussion of the relationship between pornography and rape, see Dines 2005.

2. RAPE AS SPECTATOR SPORT AND CREEPSHOT ENTERTAINMENT

1. For a discussion of the relationship between rape and manhood and masculinity, see Kimmel (2005) and Miedzian (2005) in Buchwald et al. (2005). In that same volume, Michael Messner (2005) discusses the relationship between violence toward women and sports culture.

2. See studies by Gager & Schurr 1976; Clark & Lewis 1977; Malamuth & Check 1980; Tieger 1981; and Scully & Marolla 1984.

3. Nationally, only 2 percent of men were in fraternities, but 85 percent of Fortune 500 executives, 76 percent of members of Congress, 85 percent of Supreme Court justices, and all but a few U.S. presidents and vice presidents were in the Greek system (Stein 2014).

4. Cf. Foley et al. 1995; Donovan & Williams 2002; George & Martinez 2002.

5. Cf. Archard 1998.

6. Cf. Kazan 1998.

7. Cf. Feinberg 1987; Hurd 1996; Archard 1998, 2007; Wertheimer 2003; Westen 2004; McGregor 2005.

8. See Archard 1998.

9. For a discussion of when, or whether, an unconscious woman can give consent, see Gotell 2012.

10. See MacKinnon's *Toward a Feminist Theory of the State* (1991) and Archard's *Sexual Consent* (1998) for arguments against the conflation of passivity with consent.

11. Cf. Warshaw 1994.

12. See Lisak and Miller for a discussion of repeat offenders (2002). They argue that men who rape women are more likely to have hostile attitudes toward women. In addition, they note that a culture of hypermasculinity coincides with rape tolerance. Sarah Edwards et al. (2014) recently confirmed their findings.

13. Cf. MacKinnon 1989; Gotell 2012.

14. Cf. Corteen (2004:173); see also Archard (1998:37–39).

15. See Gotell 2012.

16. See Marcus 2006; Gotell 2012.

17. See Rubenfeld 2014.

18. Heenan and Murray found 2.1 percent false reporting (2006), Kelly et al. found 2.5 percent (2005), Lonsway and Archambault found 6.8 percent (2008), and most recently Lisak et al. found 5.9 percent (2010). Although older studies report rates as high as 10.3 percent (Clark & Lewis 1977), I'm relying on studies from the last ten years. Wolitzky-Taylor et al. found only 11.5 percent of women report rapes on campus and only 2.7 percent report when drugs or alcohol is involved (2011).

19. See Benedet 2010; Gotell 2012.

20. Catharine A. MacKinnon famously argued that in a patriarchal culture under conditions of sexist oppression, women cannot *freely* consent to heterosexual sex, which under these conditions is always merely an expression of male dominance (1991).

21. There may, of course, as others have noted, be types of force other than physical force. In our patriarchal culture, there are still many forms of coercion and pressure that shape the lives of girls and women in ways that may harm them. The pressures of patriarchal expectations cloud the issue of consent. See Burgess-Jackson 1996; Jeffreys 1997; Falk 1998; Schulhofer 2000; and Whisnant 2008.

22. See Gotell 2012.

23. For example, 78-year-old Henry Rayhons was tried and acquitted for raping his wife who suffered from dementia. The question is whether or not

she was mentally competent enough to consent to sex. Health workers fall on both sides of the question. Some argue that her mental state made it impossible for her to consent. Others argue that sex is more primal than word or face recognition, that she was always happy to see her husband, and that intimacy is healthy for Alzheimer's patients (Belluck 2015). This case raises similar problems to those raised in cases of mentally impaired persons and whether or not they can consent to sex. Although we want legislation that protects vulnerable people from sexual predators, we also want to acknowledge their ability to choose and exercise agency. Cf. McCarthy and Thompson in Cowling and Reynolds, eds., *Making Sense of Sexual Consent* (2004).

24. For an excellent discussion of various shades of consent, see Archard 1998. For discussions of the relationship between rape and drugs and alcohol, see Mohler-Kuo et al. 2004, Armstrong et al. 2006, and Krebs et al. 2009.

25. For a discussion of sex crimes and prison sentencing, see Chloë Taylor 2009.

26. For a discussion of rape in the military, see Enloe 2005.

27. See Yaeger et al. 2006; and Corbett 2007.

28. Cf. Warshaw 1994:110–14. In the documentary *The Hunting Ground*, several college women share stories of being harassed after reporting rape (2015). See also Kingkade 2015.

29. See also Edwards 2013.

30. For discussions of "blame the victim" in cases of rape, see, for example, Henderson 1992, Snow 1994, Sanday 1996, Burgess-Jackson 1999, and Kingkade 2014a.

31. See Ullman & Peter-Hagene 2014.

32. For example, see Men's Rights at reddit.com; and Avoiceformalestudents. com (where one article on false reporting features a woman's lips, thick with red lipstick, with the word LIE written over them: Taylor 2014).

33. Even on the Internet Movie Database (IMDb) movie webpage for *The Hunting Ground*, the first comment is a vitriolic attack on the film: "The 'rape culture' is a marketing tool using made-up data to get more government subsidies for special interest groups' administrative salaries. It's disgusting how feminist [*sic*] use victimization for profit! . . . California's 'yes means yes' law legalizes false claims of rape" (accessed June 10, 2015).

34. This is the way bystanders and the rapists described the victim of the Steubenville (Ohio) rape and the way the juror described the video of the Vanderbilt rape victim.

35. For an insightful phenomenology of the effects of rape while unconscious or semiconscious, see Cressida Heyes's "Dead to the World: Rape, Unconsciousness, and Social Media" (2016). Heyes analyzes the importance of

the anonymity and vulnerability of sleep, which becomes impossible for women raped while asleep.

36. Cf. du Toit, 2009:82.

37. "Dear Colleague Letter" (United States Department of Education 2011). For discussions of PTSD and trauma resulting from sexual assault, and from the reporting of sexual assault, see Leiner et al. 2012; Au et al. 2013; and Ullman and Peter-Hagene 2014. These studies show that PTSD and/ or depression frequently occur in victims after sexual assault. Reactions to victim's reporting dramatically affects subsequent symptoms (Ullman & Peter-Hagene 2014).

38. See Heyes 2016.

39. See Shim 2014.

40. See Heyes 2016.

41. The topic of social media shaming has made it onto the big screen in the film *Unfriended* (2015), in which a high school girl kills herself after compromising photographs of her drunk and unconscious appear on social media. In this horror revenge fantasy, the girl gets revenge on her friends who posted the pictures without her consent.

42. "Dear Colleague Letter" (United States Department of Education 2011).

43. See also Brison 2003; Archard 2007; and Kim 2012.

44. "Many women who attended the party had the red X's on their hands, leading authorities to believe that they were part of a color-coded and premeditated plan to target certain individuals for possible date rape" (Mejia 2014).

45. Cf. Bauer 2015:77–78.

46. News reports of the Steubenville rape of a high school teenager and reports of rape of a Vanderbilt Senior include remarks by boys and men involved that make clear they considered their actions "clowning" around, or fun, and the pictures of the girls as funny (Dean 2013; Ley 2013).

47. In his *New York Times* article "Tackling the Roots of Rape," journalist Frank Bruni distills the work of Chris Kilmartin, psychology professor and author of *The Masculine Self*: "It's not DNA we're up against. It's movies, manners and a set of mores, magnified in the worlds of the military and sports, that assign different roles and different worth to men and women. . . . Its deepest roots, he [Kilmartin] said, are the cult of hypermasculinity, which tells boys that aggression is natural and sexual conquest enviable, and a set of laws and language that cast women as inferior, pliable, even disposable" (Bruni 2013). See also Messerschmidt 2000; Jensen 2007, and Jones 2013. Robert Jensen describes "dominant masculinity" as "ready to rape" and "numbed, disconnected, shut down" (Jensen 2007:1, 185). In a 2000 study, James Messerschmidt found that adolescent male sexual violence was often motivated by social pressures to prove their masculinity.

48. E.g., Estrich 1987.
49. Ibid.
50. Erdley 2014; and Coronel et al. 2015.
51. In July 2015, Vandenburg's and Batey's original trial was declared a mistrial because one of the jurors was once a party in a sexual assault case. A new trial is set for November 2015.
52. Cf. CNN Staff 2013.
53. For a philosophical delineation of differences between consent and desire, see Schulhofer's *Unwanted Sex* (2000).
54. Cf. Carmon 2013.
55. Cf. Merlan 2014; Shim 2014.
56. See College Humor 2014.
57. See "Creepshots" n.d.
58. "Clinical psychologist David Lisak trains prosecutors and police about sex offenders. His pioneering research revealed a remarkable fact. 'The vast majority of sexual assaults on campuses, in fact over 90 percent, are being perpetrated by serial offenders.' . . . Six percent of them described sexual encounters in a way that met the legal definition of rape, meaning they had sexual intercourse without the consent of the woman, often using either force or alcohol. Of that group, a majority had assaulted multiple women. 'Those serial offenders were prolific,' Lisak said. 'The average number of rapes for each one of those serial offenders was six'" (Gordon 2014). See Lisak and Miller 2002.

3. GIRLS AS PREDATORS AND PREY

1. For an extended discussion of parental figures in recent Young Adult fantasies, *The Hunger Games* in particular, see my "Ambiguity, Ambivalence, and Extravagant Love: Katniss Everdeen in *The Hunger Games*" (Oliver 2014).
2. See Do Rozario 2004; Ebersol 2014.
3. See Ebersol 2014.
4. For a discussion of the evolution of the Disney princess, see Do Rozario 2004; Bartyzel 2013; Hugel 2013; Stover 2013; Ebersol 2014; and Griffiths 2014. For a discussion of princesses and rape in the popular television show *Game of Thrones*, see Frankel 2014.
5. Cf. Do Rozario 2004.
6. For a discussion of the absent mother in fairytales, see Haas 1995. See also Livingstone and Liebes 1995; there they analyze the missing mother in soap operas and fairytales. They argue that the separation of daughter

from mother is shown as necessary and that it helps make the daughter more dependent upon men. See also Warner 1994.

7. See Oliver 2012.

8. For a sustained discussion of pregnancy and birth in *Twilight*, see Oliver 2012.

9. See Oliver 2012

CONCLUSION: THE NEW ARTEMIS, TITLE IX, AND TAKING RESPONSIBILITY FOR SEXUAL ASSAULT

1. The 1972 legislation reads: "No person in the United States shall, on the basis of sex, be excluded from participation in, be denied the benefits of, or be subjected to discrimination under any education program or activity receiving federal financial assistance." Office of the Assistant Secretary for Administration and Management, 1972. "Title IX, Education Amendments of 1972." Washington, D.C.: Department of Labor.

2. See "The Artemis Women in Action Film Festival" (n.d.).

3. See also Stimpson 2006.

4. The latest high-profile example is that of Laura Kipnis whose article in the *Chronicle of Higher Education* criticizing Northwestern University's "sexual paranoia" about relationships between students and faculty led to students protesting by carrying mattresses. See Kipnis 2015.

5. See Taylor 2009; Gotell 2012; Taylor 2013.

6. "A bipartisan group of 32 Senators has proposed the *Campus Accountability & Safety Act* to protect students and boost accountability and transparency at colleges and universities. The new legislation incorporates input from survivors, students, colleges and universities, law enforcement and advocates. It would do the following: Establish new campus resources and support services for student survivors. Ensure that college and university staff meet minimum training standards to address sexual assault cases. Create historic transparency requirements to provide students, parents and officials with an accurate picture of the problem, and of how campuses are addressing it. Require a uniform student disciplinary process across campuses, and coordination with law enforcement. Incentivize colleges and universities to address the problem by establishing enforceable Title IX penalties and stiffer penalties for Clery Act violations" (The Office of Kristin Gillibrand, n.d.).

WORKS CITED

20/20. 2015. "The Party's Over." ABC, January 30; see http://abc.go.com /shows/2020/listing/2015-01/30-2020-130-the-partys-over.

Ackerman, Spencer. 2013. "Air Force Brochure Tells Sexual Assault Victims to 'Submit.'" *Wired*, May 7; see www.wired.com/2013/05/air-force-sexual -assault-brochure/.

Adams, Carol J. 1990. *The Sexual Politics of Meat: A Feminist-Vegetarian Critical Theory.* New York: Continuum International.

———. 2003. *The Pornography of Meat.* New York: Continuum International.

Adams-Curtis, L. E. and G. B. Forbes. 2004. "College Women's Experiences of Sexual Coercion." *Trauma, Violence, and Abuse* 5: 91–122.

Aladdin. 1992. Directed by Ron Clements and John Musker. Burbank, CA: Walt Disney Studios Home Entertainment, 2015. DVD.

American Association of University Professors (AAUP), Committee A on Academic Freedom and Tenure. 2014. "On Trigger Warnings"; see www.aaup .org/report/trigger-warnings.

Anderson, Irina. 2007. "What Is a Typical Rape? Effects of Victim and Participant Gender in Female and Male Rape Perception." *British Journal of Social Psychology* 46 (1): 225–45.

Anderson, M. 2003. "Prostitution in U.S. Rape Law." *Journal of Trauma Practice* 2 (3/4): 75–92.

Anderson, Stacey. 2014. "Archery Tag Offers a Tame Version of 'The Hunger Games.'" *New York Times*, May 8; see www.nytimes.com/2014/05/09/nyregion /archery-tag-offers-a-tame-version-of-the-hunger-games.html.

Andre. 1994. Directed by George Miller. Hollywood, CA: Paramount Pictures, 2013. DVD.

Archard, David. 1997. "'A Nod's as Good as a Wink': Consent, Convention, and Reasonable Belief." *Legal Theory* 3 (3): 273–90.

——. 1998. *Sexual Consent*. Boulder, CO: Westview Press.

——. 2007. Reviews of *Is It Rape? On Acquaintance Rape and Taking Women's Consent Seriously* by Joan McGregor; *Making Sense of Sexual Consent* by Mark Cowling and Paul Reynolds; *The Logic of Consent: The Diversity and Deceptiveness of Consent as a Defence to Criminal Conduct* by Peter Westen; and *Consent to Sexual Relations* by Lan Wertheimer. *Journal of Applied Philosophy* 24 (2): 209–221.

Armstrong, Elizabeth A., Laura Hamilton, and Brian Sweeney. 2006. "Sexual Assault on Campus: A Multilevel, Integrative Approach to Party Rape." *Social Problems* 53 (4): 483–99.

"The Artemis Women in Action Film Festival." N.d. (accessed June 17, 2015); see www.artemisfilmfestival.com/.

The Associated Press. 2015. "Penn State Social Groups to Be Examined After Photo Scandal." *New York Times*, March 23; see www.nytimes.com/aponline /2015/03/23/us/ap-us-penn-state-fraternity-nude-photos.html.

Au, Teresa M., Benjamin D. Dickstein, Jonathan S. Comer, Kristalyn Salters-Pedneault, and Brett T. Litz. 2013. "Co-Occurring Posttraumatic Stress and Depression Symptoms After Sexual Assault: A Latent Profile Analysis." *Journal of Affective Disorders* 149 (1/3): 209–216.

Avatar. 2009. Directed by James Cameron. Los Angeles: 20th Century Fox, 2012. DVD.

Bachman, Melissa. 2011. "Why Every Girl Should Try Bowhunting." *Petersen's Hunting*, October 31; see www.petersenshunting.com/uncategorized /melissa-bachman-women-bowhunting/.

Barchenger, Stacey. 2015a. "Alleged Vanderbilt Rape Victim: 'That's Me' in Video." *The Tennessean*, January 28; see www.tennessean.com/story/news/2015/01/22 /alleged-vanderbilt-rape-victim-takes-stand-thats-me/22167013/.

——. 2015b. "Friends: Vandenburg Panicked, Destroyed Cellphones After Alleged Rape." *The Tennessean*, January 22; see www.tennessean.com /story/news/crime/2015/01/21/friends-vandenburg-panicked-destroyed-cell-phones-alleged-rape-vanderbilt-dorm/22143677/.

——. 2015c. "Transcripts in Vanderbilt Rape Case to Be Ready This Month." *The Tennessean*, March 13; see www.tennessean.com/story/news/crime/2015/03/13 /vanderbilt-rape-case-transcripts-mistrial-march-jury/70284186/.

Barker, Meg. 2013. "Consent Is a Grey Area? A Comparison of Understandings in *Fifty Shades of Grey* and on the BDSM Blogosphere." *Sexualities* 16 (8): 896–914.

Bartyzel, Monika. 2013. "Girls on Film: The Real Problem with the Disney Princess Brand." *The Week*, May 17; see http://theweek.com/articles/464290/girls-film-real-problem-disney-princess-brand.

Bauer, Nancy. 2015. *How to Do Things with Pornography*. Cambridge: Harvard University Press.

BBC Staff. 2015. "How a Rape Was Filmed and Shared in Pakistan." BBC, February 26; see www.bbc.com/news/world-asia-31313551.

Beauty and the Beast. 1991. Directed by Gary Trousdale and Kirk Wise. Burbank, CA: Walt Disney Pictures, 2002. DVD.

Beauvoir, Simone de. 2009 [1949]. *The Second Sex*. London: Jonathan Cape.

Bekiempis, Victoria. 2015. "When Campus Rapists Don't Think They're Rapists." *Newsweek*, January 9; see www.newsweek.com/campus-rapists-and-semantics-297463.

Belluck, Pam. 2015. "Sex, Dementia and a Husband on Trial at Age 78." *New York Times*, April 13; see www.nytimes.com/2015/04/14/health/sex-dementia-and-a-husband-henry-rayhons-on-trial-at-age-78.html.

Benedet, Janine. 2010. "The Sexual Assault of Intoxicated Women." *Canadian Journal of Women and the Law* 22 (2): 435–62.

Benedet, Janine and Isabel Grant. 2010. "R v A (J): Confusing Unconsciousness with Autonomy." *Criminal Reports* 74 (6): 80–85.

Bercovici, Jeff. 2014. "ICA Suspends Tinder Co-Founder After Sex Harassment Lawsuit." *Forbes Magazine*, July 1; see www.forbes.com/sites/jeffbercovici/2014/07/01/iac-suspends-tinder-co-founder-after-sexism-lawsuit/.

Berlant, Lauren. 1994. "America, 'Fat,' the Fetus." *boundary 2* 21 (3): 145–95.

The Birds. 1963. Directed by Alfred Hitchcock. Universal City, CA: Universal Studios, 2012. DVD.

Bleecker, E. Timothy and Sarah K. Murnan. 2005. "Fraternity Membership, the Display of Sexual Images of Women, and Rape Myth Acceptance." *Sex Roles* 53 (7/8): 487–93.

Bogle, Kathleen A. 2007. "The Shift from Dating to Hooking Up in College: What Scholars Have Missed." *Sociology Compass* 1 (2): 775–88.

———. 2008. *Hooking Up: Sex, Dating, and Relationships on Campus*. New York: NYU Press.

Bourke, Joanna. 2007. *Rape: Sex, Violence, History*. Berkeley, CA: Counterpoint.

Brave. 2012. Directed by Mark Andrews and Brenda Chapman. Burbank, CA: Walt Disney Studios Motion Pictures, 2012. DVD.

Brison, Susan J. 2003. *Aftermath: Violence and the Remaking of a Self*. Princeton, NJ: Princeton University Press.

The Brood. 1979. Directed by David Cronenberg. Beverly Hills, CA: MGM, 2003. DVD.

Brook, Tom Vanden and Gregg Zoroya. 2013. "Why the Military Hasn't Stopped Sexual Abuse." *USA Today*, May 15; see www.usatoday.com/story /news/2013/05/15/why-the-military-hasnt-stopped-sexual-abuse-/2162399/.

Brownmiller, Susan. 1975. *Against Our Will: Men, Women, and Rape.* New York: Simon and Schuster.

Bruni, Frank. 2013. "Tackling the Roots of Rape." *New York Times*, August 12; see www.nytimes.com/2013/08/13/opinion/bruni-tackling-the-roots-of-rape .html.

Buchwald, Emilie, Pamela Fletcher, Martha Roth, eds. 2005. *Transforming a Rape Culture.* Minneapolis: Milkweed Editions.

Burnett, Ann, Jody L. Mattern, Liliana L. Herakova, David H. Kahl, Cloy Tobola, and Susan E. Bornsen. 2009. "Communicating/Muting Date Rape: A Co-Cultural Theoretical Analysis of Communication Factors Related to Rape Culture on a College Campus." *Journal of Applied Communication Research* 37 (4): 465–85.

Burgess-Jackson, Keith. 1996. *Rape: A Philosophical Investigation.* Brookfield, VT: Dartmouth.

Burgess-Jackson, Keith, ed. 1999. *A Most Detestable Crime: New Philosophical Essays on Rape.* New York: Oxford University Press.

Cahill, Ann J. 2001. *Rethinking Rape.* Ithaca: Cornell University Press.

Carey, Kate B., Sarah E. Durney, Robyn L. Shepardson, and Michael P. Carey. 2015. "Incapacitated and Forcible Rape of College Women: Prevalence Across the First Year." *Journal of Adolescent Health* 56 (6): 678–80.

Caringella, S. 2008. *Addressing Rape Reform in Law and Practice.* New York: Columbia University Press.

Carmon, Irin. 2013. "Rape in the Age of Social Media." *Salon*, January 10; see www.salon.com/2013/01/10/rape_in_the_age_of_social_media/.

Carrie. 1976. Directed by Brian De Palma. Beverly Hills, CA: MGM, 2001. DVD.

Carrie. 2013. Directed by Kimberly Peirce. Los Angeles: 20th Century Fox, 2014. DVD.

Caruso, Kevin. N.d. "Rape Victims Prone to Suicide," Suicide.org; see www.suicide .org/rape-victims-prone-to-suicide.html.

Cat People. 1942. Directed by Jacques Tourneur. Atlanta: Turner Home Entertainment, 2005. DVD.

Christina, Greta. 1997. "Are We Having Sex Now or What?" In Alan Soble, ed., *The Philosophy of Sex*, 3–8. Lanham, MD: Rowman and Littlefield.

Cinderella. 1950. Directed by Clyde Geronimi, Hamilton Luske, and Wilfred Jackson. Burbank, CA: Walt Disney Productions, 2012. DVD.

Cinderella. 2015. Directed by Kenneth Branagh. Burbank, CA: Walt Disney Studios. Film.

Clark, L. and D. Lewis. 1977. *Rape: The Price of Coercive Sexuality.* Toronto: Women's Press.

CNN Staff. 2013. "Convicted Steubenville Teen Classified as a Sex Offender." CNN, June 15; see www.cnn.com/2013/06/14/justice/ohio-steubenville-sex -offender/index.html.

College Humor. 2014. "Tinderella: A Modern Fairy Tale." *YouTube*, January 29; see www.youtube.com/watch?v=bLoRPielarA.

Collins, Suzanne. 2010. *The Hunger Games.* New York: Scholastic Press.

———. 2013. *Catching Fire.* New York: Scholastic Press.

———. 2014. *Mockingjay.* New York: Scholastic Press.

Corbett, Sara. 2007. "The Women's War." *New York Times Magazine*, March 18; see www.nytimes.com/2007/03/18/magazine/18cover.html?pagewanted=all.

Coronel, Sheila, David Coll, and Derek Kravitz. 2015. " 'A Rape on Campus': What Went Wrong?" *Rolling Stone*, April 5; see www.rollingstone.com/culture /features/a-rape-on-campus-20141119.

Corteen, Karen. 2004. "Beyond (Hetero)sexual Consent." In Cowling and Reynolds, eds., *Making Sense of Sexual Consent*, 171–94.

Cowling, Mark and Paul Reynolds, eds. 2004. *Making Sense of Sexual Consent.* Burlington, VT: Ashgate.

"Creepshots." N.d. *Metareddit* (accessed April 22, 2015); see http://metareddit .com/r/CreepShots/.

Culkin, Tommy. 2015. "New Consent Apps Aim to Combat Campus Rape." *The Appalachian Online*, March 31; see http://theappalachianonline.com /2015/03/31/new-consent-apps-aim-to-combat-campus-rape/.

Cuthbertson, Richard. 2015. "Internet Porn 'Rewiring' Young Brains, Halifax Therapists Say." CBC, January 2; see www.cbc.ca/m/touch/canada/nova -scotia/story/1.2888603.

Davies, Michelle and Paul Rogers. 2006. "Perceptions of Male Victims in Depicted Sexual Assaults: A Review of the Literature." *Aggression and Violent Behavior* 11 (4): 367–77.

Deadgirl. 2008. Directed by Marcel Sarmiento and Gadi Harel. Chicago: Dark Sky Films, 2009. DVD.

Dean, Michelle. 2013. "The Lessons of Steubenville." *The New Yorker*, January 11; see www.newyorker.com/culture/culture-desk/the-lessons-of-steubenville.

Dewan, Shaila and Sheryl Gay Stolberg. 2015. "University of Mary Washington, Where Woman Was Killed, Faces Scrutiny." *New York Times*, May 6; see www.nytimes.com/2015/05/07/us/university-of-mary-washington-where -woman-was-killed-faces-scrutiny.html.

Dines, Gail. 2005. "Unmasking the Pornography Industry: From Fantasy to Reality." In Buchwald et al., eds., *Transforming a Rape Culture*, 105–115.

Divergent. 2014. Directed by Neil Burger. Santa Monica, CA: Lionsgate, 2014. DVD.

"Divergent: Tris' Fear Simulation Test." 2013. *YouTube*, July 23; see www.youtube .com/watch?v=GKfwLeZDEEU.

The Divergent Series: Insurgent. 2015. Directed by Robert Schwentke. Santa Monica, CA: Lionsgate. Film.

Donovan, R. and M. Williams. 2002. "Living at the Intersection: The Effects of Racism and Sexism on Black Rape Survivors." *Women & Therapy* 3–4 (25): 95–105.

Do Rozario, Rebecca-Anne. 2004. "The Princess and the Magic Kingdom: Beyond Nostalgia, the Function of the Disney Princess." *Women's Studies in Communication* 27 (1): 34–59.

Duncan, Margaret Carlisle. 2006. "The Promise of Artemis." S&F Online 4 (3); see http://sfonline.barnard.edu/sport/duncan_01.htm.

du Toit, Louise. 2009. *A Philosophical Investigation of Rape: The Making and Unmaking of the Feminine Self*. New York: Routledge.

Dymock, Alex. 2013. "Flogging Sexual Transgression: Interrogating the Costs of the '*Fifty Shades* Effect.'" *Sexualities* 16 (8): 880–95.

Ebersol, Kaitlin. 2014. "How Fourth Wave Feminism Is Changing Disney's Princesses." *Highbrow Magazine*, October 23; see www.highbrowmagazine .com/4388-how-fourth-wave-feminism-changing-disney-s-princesses.

The Economist. 2006. "Sisters Are Killing It for Themselves," January 5; see www.economist.com/node/5364819.

Edwards, David. 2013. "CNN Grieves That Guilty Verdict Ruined 'Promising' Lives of Steubenville Rapists." *Raw Story*, March 17; see www.rawstory .com/2013/03/cnn-grieves-that-guilty-verdict-ruined-promising-lives-of-steubenville-rapists/.

Edwards Sarah R., Kathryn A. Bradshaw, and Verlin B. Hinsz. 2014. "Denying Rape But Endorsing Forceful Intercourse." *Violence and Gender* 1 (4): 188–93.

Elbert, Thomas, Roland Weierstall, and Maggie Schauer. 2010. "Fascination Violence: On Mind and Brain of Man Hunters." *European Archives of Psychiatry and Clinical Neuroscience* 260 (2): 100–105.

Enchanted. 2007. Directed by Kevin Lima. Burbank, CA: Walt Disney Studios Home Entertainment, 2008. DVD.

Enloe, Cynthia. 2005. "Maneuvers: When Soldiers Rape." In Buchwald et al., eds., *Transforming a Rape Culture*,117–20.

Erdley, Sabrina Rubin. 2014. "A Rape on Campus: A Brutal Assault and Struggle for Justice at UVA." *Rolling Stone*, November 19; see http://web .archive.org/web/20141120205928/http://www.rollingstone.com/culture /features/a-rape-on-campus-20141119.

Estrich, Susan. 1987. *Real Rape*. Cambridge: Harvard University Press.

Fagan, Kate and Jane McManus. 2015. "OK, We Really Need to Talk About 'The Hunting Ground.'" *espnW.com*, March 16; see http://espn.go.com/espnw /news-commentary/article/12491771/ok-really-need-talk-hunting-ground.

Falk, P. 1998. "Rape by Fraud and Rape by Coercion." *Brooklyn Law Review* 64: 39–180.

Feinberg, Joel. 1987. *Harm to Others*. New York: Oxford University Press.

Fifty Shades of Grey. 2015. Directed by Sam Taylor-Johnson. Universal City, CA: Universal Pictures, 2015. DVD.

Filipovic, Jill. 2014. "Two Years Ago, a Woman Was Sexually Assaulted While Sleeping on the Subway and a Video Went Viral. Now She's Speaking Out." *Cosmopolitan*, December 24; see www.cosmopolitan.com/politics/news /a34627/subway-sexual-assault/.

——. 2015. "Most College Presidents Believe Sexual Assault Isn't a Problem on Their Campuses." *Cosmopolitan*, March 18.

Finch, Emily and Vanessa Munro. 2007. "The Demon Drink and the Demonized Woman: Socio-Sexual Stereotypes and Responsibility Attribution in Rape Trials Involving Intoxicants." *Social Legal Studies* 16: 591.

Finn, Natalie. 2015. "Jennifer Lawrence Slammed by PETA for Squirrel-Skinning Joke (and Saying Screw PETA)." *E! Online*; see www.eonline.com /news/307761/jennifer-lawrence-slammed-by-peta-for-squirrel-skinning -joke-and-saying-screw-peta.

Fisher, Bonnie S., Francis T. Cullen, and Michael G. Turner. 2000. "The Sexual Victimization of College Women." Research Report. Washington, D.C.: National Institute of Justice, Bureau of Justice Statistics.

Fitzgerald, Amy J. 2005. "The Emergence of the Figure of 'Woman-The-Hunter': Equality or Complicity in Oppression?" *Women's Studies Quarterly* 33 (1/2): 86–104.

Foley, L. A., C. Evanic, K. Karnik, J. King, and A. Parks. 1995. "Date Rape Effects of Race and Assailant and Victim and Gender on Subjects and Perceptions." *Journal of Black Psychology* 21: 6–18.

Forbes, Gordon B., Leah E. Adams-Curtis, Alexis H. Pakalka, and Kay B. White. 2006. "Dating Aggression, Sexual Coercion, and Aggression-Supporting Attitudes Among College Men as a Function of Participation in Aggressive High School Sports." *Violence Against Women* 12 (5): 441–55.

FoxNews.com. 2013. "US Sees 25 Percent Surge in Women Hunters Since 2006." *FoxNews.com*, November 10; see www.foxnews.com/sports/2013/11/10/us -sees-25-percent-surge-in-women-hunters-since-2006/.

Frampton, Pam. 2015. "Girls on Film." *The Telegram* (England), March 21; see www.thetelegram.com/Opinion/Columnists/2015-03-21/article-4084203 /Girls-on-film/1.

Franke-Ruta, Garance, 2012. "A Canard That Will Not Die: 'Legitimate Rape' Doesn't Cause Pregnancy." *The Atlantic*, August 19.

Frankel, Valerie Estelle. 2014. *Women in Game of Thrones: Power, Conformity, and Resistance*. Jefferson, NC: McFarland.

Freitas, Donna. 2013. *The End of Sex: How Hookup Culture Is Leaving a Generation Unhappy, Sexually Unfulfilled, and Confused About Intimacy*. New York: Basic Books.

Frozen. 2013. Directed by Chris Buck and Jennifer Lee. Burbank, CA: Walt Disney Studios Motion Pictures, 2014. DVD.

Fuchs, Erin, Michael B. Kelley, and Gus Lubin. 2013. "Social Media Makes Teen Rape More Traumatic Than Ever." *Business Insider*, April 12; see www.businessinsider.com/the-impact-of-social-media-on-rape-2013-4.

Gaarder, Emily. 2011. "Where the Boys Aren't: The Predominance of Women in Animal Rights Activism." *Feminist Formations* 23 (2): 54–76.

Gager, H. and C. Schurr. 1976. *Sexual Assault: Confronting Rape in America*. New York: Grosset and Dunlap.

Garrity, Meghan and Alan Blinder. 2015. "Penn State Fraternity's Secret Facebook Photos May Lead to Criminal Charges." *New York Times*, March 17; see www.nytimes.com/2015/03/18/us/penn-state-fraternitys-secret-facebook-photos-may-lead-to-criminal-charges.html.

Gartner, Lisa. 2013. "At 'Hunger Games' Camp, Children Want to Fight to the 'Death.'" *Tampa Bay Times*, August 2; see www.tampabay.com/news/humaninterest/at-hunger-games-camp-children-want-to-fight-to-the-death/2134621.

George, W. H. and L. J. Martinez. 2002. "Victim-Blaming in Rape Effects of Victim and Perpetrator Race, Type of Rape, and Participant Racism." *Psychology of Women Quarterly* 26: 110–19.

"The Girl Who Cries Home." 2012. *America's Next Top Model: College Edition (Cycle 19)*. Directed by Tony Croll. The CW; see www.youtube.com/watch?v=AMJe6krZgoI.

The Girl with the Dragon Tattoo. 2011. Directed by David Fincher. Los Angeles: Columbia Pictures, 2012. DVD.

Glenza, Jessica and Rory Carroll. 2015. "Stanford, the Swimmer and Yik Yak: Can Talk of Campus Rape Go Beyond Secrets?" *The Guardian* (England), February 8; see www.theguardian.com/society/2015/feb/08/stanford-swimmer-yik-yak-campus-rape.

Glock, Allison. 2015. "Fighting Rape on Campus: Talking with Two Heroes from 'The Hunting Ground.'" espnW, April 29; see http://espn.go.com/espnw/athletes-life/article/12776315/.

Goldberg, Michelle. 2014. "Questions About California's New Campus Rape Law." *The Nation*, September 29; see www.thenation.com/blog/181787/questions-about-californias-new-campus-rape-law.

Gordon, Claire. 2014. "Why Don't We Talk About All the Serial Rapists?" *Al Jazeera America*, March 14; see http://america.aljazeera.com/watch/shows/america-tonight/america-tonight-blog/2014/3/14/why-don-t-we-talkaboutalltheserialrapists.html.

Gotell, Lise. 2008. "Rethinking Affirmative Consent in Canadian Sexual Assault Law: Neoliberal Sexual Subjects and Risky Women." *Akron Law Review* 41: 865–98.

——. 2010. "Canadian Sexual Assault Law: Neoliberalism and the Erosion of Feminist-Inspired Law Reforms." In Clare McGlynn and Vanessa E. Munro, eds., *Rethinking Rape Law: International and Comparative Perspectives*, 209–223. New York: Routledge.

——. 2012. "Governing Heterosexuality Through Specific Consent: Interrogating the Governmental Effects of R. v J.A." *Canadian Journal of Women and Law* 24: 359–88.

Greco, Patti. 2011. "Joe Wright on His Feminist, Fairy-Tale-Inspired Action Movie, *Hanna*." *Vulture*, April 7; see www.vulture.com/2011/04/joe_wright_on_his_feminist-fai.html.

Green, Emma. 2015. "Fifty Shades of Grey Gets BDSM Dangerously Wrong." *The Atlantic*, February 10; see www.theatlantic.com/features/archive/2015/02/consent-isnt-enough-in-fifty-shades-of-grey/385267/.

Griffiths, Kadeen. 2014. "Disney's 'Moana' Could Do for Diversity What 'Frozen' Did for Feminist Leads, If They Do It Right." *Bustle*. August 19; see www.bustle.com/articles/36353-disneys-moana-could-do-for-diversity-what-frozen-did-for-feminist-leads-if-they-do-it.

Grinberg, Emanuella. 2013. "When Evidence Goes Viral." CNN, April 16; see www.cnn.com/2013/04/12/living/social-media-evidence-sexual-assault/.

Gross, Doug. 2013. "Why People Share Murder, Rape on Facebook—CNN.com." CNN, August 9; see www.cnn.com/2013/08/09/tech/social-media/crime-social-media-psychology/index.html.

Haas, Lynda. 1995. " 'Eighty-Six the Mother': Murder, Matricide, and Good Mothers." In E. Bell, L. Hass, and L. Sells, eds., *From Mouse to Mermaid: The Politics of Film, Gender, and Culture*, 193–211. Bloomington: Indiana University Press.

Hamilton, Margaret and Jack Yee. 1990. "Rape Knowledge and Propensity to Rape." *Journal of Research in Personality* 24 (1): 111–22.

Hanna. 2011. Directed by Joe Wright. Universal City, CA: Focus Features, 2011. DVD.

Hasty, Katie. 2015. "Oral Sex, Condoms, and *Fifty Shades of Grey:* How the Film Did the Deed Differently." *Hit Fix*, February 16; see www .hitfix.com/immaculate-noise/how-fifty-shades-of-grey-did-onscreen -sex-differently-or-even-right.

Heenan, M. and S. Murray. 2006. *Study of Reported Rapes in Victoria, 2000–2003.* Melbourne, Australia: Office of Women's Policy, Department for Victorian Communities.

Henderson, Lynne. 1992. "Rape and Responsibility." *Law and Philosophy* 11 (1/2): 127–78.

Heyes, Cressida J. 2016. "Dead to the World: Rape, Unconsciousness, and Social Media." *Signs: Journal of Women in Culture and Society* 40 (1).

Higgins, Lynn A. and Brenda R. Silver, eds. 1991. *Rape and Representation.* New York: Columbia University Press.

The Hobbit: Desolation of Smaug. 2013. Directed by Peter Jackson. Burbank, CA: Warner Brothers Pictures. 2014. DVD.

Holley, Peter. 2015. "College Student Accused of Rape Claims He Was Reenacting 'Fifty Shades of Grey.'" *Washington Post*, February 23; see www .washingtonpost.com/news/morning-mix/wp/2015/02/23/college-student -accused-of-rape-claims-he-was-reenacting-50-shades-of-grey/.

Hood, Grace. 2013. "More Girls Target Archery, Inspired by 'The Hunger Games.'" *NPR.org*, November 27; see www.npr.org/2013/11/27/247379498 /more-girls-target-archery-inspired-by-the-hunger-games.

Houston, M. and C. Kramarae. 1994. "Gender, Power and Miscommunication." In Camille Roman, Suzanne Juhasz, and Cristanne Miller, eds., *The Women and Language Debate: A Sourcebook*, 383–406. New Brunswick, NJ: Rutgers University Press.

Hu, Elise. 2014. "Snapchat CEO's Emails Didn't Disappear, Come Back to Shame Him." *NPR.org*, May 28; see www.npr.org/blogs/alltechconsidered /2014/05/28/316715640/snapchat-ceos-emails-didnt-disappear-come-back -to-shame-him.

Hugel, Melissa. 2013. "How Disney Princesses Went from Passive Damsels to Active Heroes." *Mic*, November 12; see http://mic.com/articles/73093 /how-disney-princesses-went-from-passive-damsels-to-active-heroes.

The Hunger Games. 2012. Directed by Gary Ross. Santa Monica, CA: Lionsgate, 2012. DVD.

The Hunger Games: Catching Fire. 2013. Directed by Francis Lawrence. Santa Monica, CA: Lionsgate, 2014. DVD.

The Hunger Games: Mockingjay—Part 1. 2014. Directed by Francis Lawrence. Santa Monica, CA: Lionsgate, 2015. DVD.

"The Hunger Games: Mockingjay Part 2, Official Trailer—'We March Together.'" 2015. *YouTube*; see www.youtube.com/watch?v=n-7K_OjsDCQ.

The Hunting Ground. 2015. *IMDB* (accessed June 10, 2015); see www.imdb
.com/title/tt4185572/.

The Hunting Ground (documentary film). 2015. Directed by Kirby Dick. New
York: The Weinstein Company.

Hurd, H. M.. 1996. "The Moral Magic of Consent." *Legal Theory* 2: 121–46.

James, E. L. 2011. *Fifty Shades of Grey*. New York: Vintage Books.

——. 2012a. *Fifty Shades Darker*. New York: Vintage Books.

——. 2012b. *Fifty Shades Freed*. New York: Vintage Books.

Jeffreys, S. 1997. *The Idea of Prostitution*. North Melbourne, Australia: Spinifex
Press.

Jensen, Robert. 2007. *Getting Off: Pornography and the End of Masculinity*.
Cambridge, MA: South End Press.

Jones, Steve. 2013. "Gender Monstrosity: *Deadgirl* and the Sexual Politics of
Zombie-Rape." *Feminist Media Studies* 13 (3): 525–39.

Jozkowski, Kristen and Zoë Peterson. 2014. "Assessing the Validity and Reliabil-
ity of the Perceptions of the Consent to Sex Scale." *Journal of Sex Research*
51 (6): 632–45.

Kang, Inkoo. 2012. "Seriously, Ladies—What's with the Arrows?" *BoxOf-
fice: The Business of Movies*, June 20; see http://pro.boxoffice.com/articles
/2012–06-the-graceful-weapon.

Kazan, Patricia. 1998. "Sexual Assault and the Problem of Consent." In Stanley
G. French, Wanda Teays, and Laura Martha Purdy, eds., *Violence Against
Women: Philosophical Perspectives*, 27–42. Ithaca: Cornell University Press.

Kelly, L., J. Lovett, and L. Regan. 2005. *A Gap or Chasm? Attrition in Reported
Rape Cases* (Home Office Research Study 293). London: Home Office
Research, Development and Statistics Directorate.

Kick-Ass. 2010. Directed by Matthew Vaughn. Santa Monica, CA: Lionsgate,
2010. DVD.

Kick-Ass 2. 2013. Directed by Jeff Wadlow. Universal City, CA: Universal Pictures, 2013. DVD.

Kilmartin, Christopher. 1994. *The Masculine Self*. New York: Macmillan.

Kimmel, Michael. 2005. "Men, Masculinity, and Rape Culture." In Buchwald
et al., eds., *Transforming a Rape Culture*, 139–58.

King Arthur. 2004. Directed by Antoine Fuqua. Burbank, CA: Buena Vista Pictures, 2004. DVD.

Kingkade, Tyler. 2014a. "Fewer Than One-Third of Campus Sexual Assault Cases
Result in Expulsion." *Huffington Post*, September 29; see www.huffingtonpost
.com/2014/09/29/campus-sexual-assault_n_5888742.html.

——. 2014b. "Why It Really Matters When College Officials Say Terrible Things
About Rape." *Huffington Post*, November 18; see www.huffingtonpost
.com/2014/11/18/college-officials-rape-things-they-say_n_6173254.html.

———. 2015. "The Bigger Problem Behind Retaliation Students Face for Reporting Sexist Behavior." *Huffington Post*, June 6; see www.huffingtonpost.com /2015/06/04/retaliation-sexist-behavior-students-colleges_n_7455556.html ?utm_hp_ref=breakingthesilence.

Kingsman: The Secret Service. 2015. Directed by Matthew Vaughn. Los Angeles: 20th Century Fox, 2015. DVD.

Kim, Jane. 2012. "Taking Rape Seriously: Rape as Slavery." *Harvard Journal of Law and Gender* 35: 263–310.

Kipnis, Laura. 2015. "Sexual Paranoia Strikes Academe." *The Chronicle of Higher Education*, February 27; see http://chronicle.com/article/Sexual -Paranoia/190351/.

Krebs, Christopher P., Christine H. Lindquist, Tara D. Warner, Bonnie S. Fisher, and Sandra L. Martin. 2009. "College Women's Experiences with Physically Forced, Alcohol- or Other Drug-Enabled, and Drug-Facilitated Sexual Assault Before and Since Entering College (Survey)." *Journal of American College Health* 57 (6): 639.

Lanfreschi, Anna. "A Real-Life 'Hunger Games' in Michigan?" 2012. *HLNtv.com*, March 6; see www.hlntv.com/article/2012/03/02/children-under-10-allowed -hunt-michigan.

Laqueur, Thomas. 1992. *Making Sex: Bodies and Gender from the Greeks to Freud*. Cambridge: Harvard University Press.

Lawrence, Quil and Marissa Peñaloza. 2013. "Sexual Violence Victims Say Military Justice System is 'Broken.'" NPR, March 21; see www.npr .org/2013/03/21/174840895/sexual-violence-victims-say-military-justice -system-is-broken.

Léglu, Catherine E. 2010. *Multilingualism and Mother Tongue in Medieval French, Occitan, and Catalan Narratives*. University Park, PA: Penn State University Press.

Leiner, Amy S., Megan C. Kearns, Joan L. Jackson, Millie C. Astin, and Barbara O. Rothbaum. 2012. "Avoidant Coping and Treatment Outcome in Rape-Related Posttraumatic Stress Disorder." *Journal of Consulting and Clinical Psychology* 80 (2): 317–21.

Ley, Tom. 2012. "How an Alleged Rape Involving Ohio High School Football Players Unfolded on Twitter, Instagram, and YouTube." *Deadspin*, December 17; see http://deadspin.com/how-an-alleged-rape-involving-ohio -high-school-football-5969103.

———. 2013. " 'She Is So Raped Right Now': Partygoer Jokes About the Steubenville Accuser the Night of the Alleged Rape." *Deadspin*, January 2; see http://deadspin.com/5972527/she-is-so-raped-right-now-former-student -jokes-about-the-steubenville-accuser-the-night-of-the-alleged-rape.

Lisak, David, Lori Gardinier, Sarah C. Nicksa, and Ashley M. Cote. 2010. "False
Allegations of Sexual Assault: An Analysis of Ten Years of Reported Cases."
Violence Against Women 16 (12): 1318–34.

Lisak, David and Paul M. Miller. 2002. "Repeat Rape and Multiple Offending
Among Undetected Rapists." *Violence and Victims* 17 (1): 73–85.

The Little Mermaid. 1989. Directed by Ron Clements and John Musker. Burbank, CA: Walt Disney Productions, 2013. DVD.

Livingstone, Sonia and Tamar Liebes. 1995. "Where Have All the Mothers
Gone? Soap Opera's Replaying of the Oedipal Story." *Critical Studies in
Mass Communication* 12 (2): 155–75.

Lonsway, K. A. and J. Archambault. 2008. "Understanding the Criminal Justice
Response to Sexual Assault: Analysis of Data from the Making a Difference
Project." Unpublished manuscript.

MacKinnon, Catharine A. 1989. *Feminism Unmodified: Discourses on Life and
Law*. Cambridge: Harvard University Press.

——. 1991. *Toward a Feminist Theory of the State*. Cambridge: Harvard University Press.

Malamuth, N. M. and J. V. P. Check. 1980. "Penile Tumescence and Perceptual Responses to Reactions." *Journal of Applied Social Psychology* 10 (6):
528–47.

Maleficent. 2014. Directed by Robert Stromberg. Burbank, CA: Walt Disney
Home Pictures, 2014. DVD.

Marcotte, Amanda. 2014a. "Do Not Fear California's New Affirmative Consent
Law." *Slate*, September 29; see www.slate.com/blogs/xx_factor/2014/09/29
/affirmative_consent_in_california_gov_jerry_brown_signs_the_yes
_means_yes.html.

——. 2014b. "Todd Akin: 'Legitimate Rape' Doesn't Result in Conception,
Unless You're One of My Staffers." *Slate*, July 17; see www.slate.com/blogs
/xx_factor/2014/07/17/todd_akin_on_msnbc_a_number_of_people_on
_my_staff_were_conceived_by_rape.html.

Marcus, Sharon. 2006. "Fighting Bodies, Fighting Words: A Theory and Politics
of Rape Prevention." In Elizabeth Hackett and Sally Haslanger, eds., *Theorizing Feminisms: A Reader*, 368–81. New York: Oxford University Press.

Marnie. 1964. Directed by Alfred Hitchcock. Universal City, CA: Universal Studios, 2006. DVD.

Martin, Amber. 2013. "Fifty Shades of Sex Shop: Sexual Fantasy for Sale." *Sexualities* 16 (8): 980–84.

McCarthy, Meghan. 2014. "I Fought Back Against My College's Sexist Fraternity." *The Atlantic*, February 24; see www.theatlantic.com/education
/archive/2014/02/i-fought-back-against-my-colleges-sexist-fraternity/284040/.

McCarthy, Michelle and Paul Reynolds. 2004. "People with Learning Disabilities: Sex, the Law, and Consent." In Cowling and Reynolds, eds., *Making Sense of Sexual Consent*, 227–42.

McCarthy, Michelle and David Thompson. 2004. "People with Learning Disabilities: Sex, the Law and Consent." In Cowling and Reynolds, eds., *Making Sense of Sexual Consent*, 227–42.

McCue, Margi Laird. 2008. *Domestic Violence: A Reference Handbook*. Santa Barbara, CA: ABC-CLIO.

McEnrue, Eva and Mel Owens. 2014. "#ShareaCondom Campaign Proves (Safe) Sex Sells." *Huffington Post*, October 23; see www.huffingtonpost.com /eva-mcenrue-mel-owens/shareacondom-campaign-pro_b_6037828.html.

McGowan, Molly. 2013. "Life Imitates Art: 'Hunger Games' Sparks Interest by Young Women in Bows and Arrows." *The [London] Times News*, November 20; see www.thetimesnews.com/news/top-news/life-imitates-art-hunger -games-sparks-interest-by-young-women-in-bows-and-arrows-1.237728.

McGregor, Joan. 2005. *Is It Rape? On Acquaintance Rape and Taking Women's Consent Seriously*. Aldershot, Hampshire, Eng.; and Burlington, VT: Ashgate.

Mejia, Paula. 2014. "University of Wisconsin–Milwaukee Fraternity Suspended, Investigated Over Date Rape Plot." *Newsweek*, September 21; see www .newsweek.com/fraternity-suspended-alleged-date-rape-plot-272072.

Merlan, Anna. 2015. "Why Were Three Teenage Rape Victims Bullied Out of School in Oklahoma?" *Jezebel* (accessed October 22); see http://jezebel.com /why-were-three-teenage-rape-victims-bullied-out-of-scho-1659721302.

Messerschmidt, James W. 2000. "Becoming 'Real Men': Adolescent Masculinity Challenges and Sexual Violence." *Men and Masculinities* 2 (3): 286–307.

Messner, Michael. 2005. "The Triad of Violence in Men's Sports." In Buchwald et al., eds., *Transforming a Rape Culture*, 23–46.

Meyer, Stephenie. 2005. *Twilight*. New York: Little, Brown.

———. 2006. *New Moon*. New York: Little, Brown.

———. 2007. *Eclipse*. New York: Little, Brown.

———. 2008. *Breaking Dawn*. New York: Little, Brown.

Miedzian, Myriam. 2005. "How Rape Is Encouraged in American Boys and What We Can Do to Stop It." In Buchwald et al., eds., *Transforming a Rape Culture*, 159–72.

Mohler-Kuo, Meichun, George W. Dowdall, Mary P. Koss, and Henry Wechsler. 2004. "Correlates of Rape While Intoxicated in a National Sample of College Women." *Journal of Studies on Alcohol* 65 (1): 37–45.

Morgan, Maybelle. 2015. "Confessions of a Tinderella." *DailyMail.com*, May 18; see www.dailymail.co.uk/femail/article-3082924/Confessions-serial-online -dater-Tinderella-s-searching-Mr-Right.html.

Mulan. 1998. Directed by Barry Cook and Tony Bancroft. Burbank, CA: Walt Disney Video, 2004. DVD.

Mulrine, Anna. 2012. "On the Front Lines of Sexual Assault in the Military: Army Chaplains." *Christian Science Monitor*, January 10; see www .csmonitor.com/USA/Military/2012/0110/On-the-front-lines-of-sexual -assault-in-the-military-Army-chaplains.

Munro, Vanessa. 2008. "Constructing Consent: Legislating Freedom and Legitimating Constraint in the Expression of Sexual Autonomy." *Akron Law Review* 21 (4): 923–56.

National Velvet. 1944. Directed by Clarence Brown. Burbank, CA: Warner Home Video, 2000. DVD.

Natsuaki, Misaki N., Leslie D. Leve, and Jane Mendle. 2011. "Going Through the Rites of Passage: Timing and Transition of Menarche, Childhood Sexual Abuse, and Anxiety Symptoms in Girls." *Journal of Youth and Adolescence* 40 (10): 1357–70.

Nim's Island. 2008. Directed by Jennifer Flackett and Mark Levin. Los Angeles, CA: 20th Century Fox, 2008. DVD.

O'Connell, Oliver. 2015. "Frat Boy DEFENDS Sickening Posts of Nude Passed Out Female Students." *Mail Online*, March 18; see www.dailymail.co.uk /news/article-3001902/Frat-Facebook-group-member-DEFENDS-sickening -posts-nude-passed-female-students-boasts-banging-lol-come-light.html.

Office of the Assistant Secretary for Administration and Management. 1972. "Title IX, Education Amendments of 1972." Washington, D.C.: Department of Labor; see www.dol.gov/oasam/regs/statutes/titleIX.htm.

The Office of Kristin Gillibrand. N.d. "Resource Center: Campus Accountability and Safety Act" (accessed June 16, 2015); see www.gillibrand.senate.gov /campus-sexual-assault.

Oliver, Kelly, 2001. *Witnessing: Beyond Recognition*. Minneapolis: University of Minnesota Press.

——. 2004. *The Colonization of Psychic Space*. Minneapolis: University of Minnesota Press.

——. 2007. *Women as Weapons of War: Iraq, Sex, and the Media*. New York: Columbia University Press.

——. 2012. *Knock Me Up, Knock Me Down: Images of Pregnancy in Hollywood Films*. New York: Columbia University Press.

——. 2013. "Hunting Girls: Patriarchal Fantasy or Feminist Progress?" *Americana: The Journal of American Popular Culture* 12 (1).

——. 2014. "Ambiguity, Ambivalence, and Extravagant Love: Katniss Everdeen in *The Hunger Games*." In *Humanities: New Encounters Between Literature and Philosophy* 3 (4): 675–86.

———. 2015. "Witnessing, Recognition, and Response Ethics," in *Philosophy and Rhetoric* 45 (4): 473–93.

Orr, Christopher. 2015. "Fifty Shades of Dull." *The Atlantic*, February 13; see www.theatlantic.com/entertainment/archive/2015/02/fifty-shades-of-grey-review/385465/.

Pitch Perfect 2. 2015. Directed by Elizabeth Banks. Universal City, CA: Universal Pictures. Film.

Pocahontas. 1995. Directed by Mike Gabriel and Eric Goldberg. Burbank, CA: Walt Disney Studios Home Entertainment, 2005. DVD.

Projansky, Sarah. 2001a. "The Elusive/Ubiquitous Representation of Rape: A Historical Survey of Rape in U.S. Film, 1903–1972." *Cinema Journal* 41 (1): 63–90.

———. 2001b. *Watching Rape*. New York: NYU Press.

Q13 Fox News Staff. 2015. "Suspect in Subway Sexual Assault Caught on Video Is Arrested 2 1/2 Years Later." Q13 FOX News, March 26; see http://q13fox .com/2015/03/26/suspect-in-subway-sexual-assault-caught-on-video-is -arrested-2-1/2-years-later/.

Reynolds, Bridget M. and Jaana Juvonen. 2011. "The Role of Early Maturation, Perceived Popularity, and Rumors in the Emergence of Internalizing Symptoms Among Adolescent Girls." *Journal of Youth and Adolescence* 40 (11): 1407–22.

———. 2012. "Pubertal Timing Fluctuations Across Middle School: Implications for Girls' Psychological Health." *Journal of Youth and Adolescence* 41 (6): 677–90.

Robbins, Alexandra. 2015. "How Sorority Culture Contributes to the Campus Rape Problem." *Washington Post*, January 30; see www.washingtonpost .com/posteverything/wp/2015/01/30/how-sorority-culture-contributes-to -the-campus-rape-problem/.

Rosenberg, Adam. 2011. "Star Saoirse Ronan on *Hanna*'s Grim Grimm's Fairy Tale." *Spinoff*, April 8; see http://spinoff.comicbookresources.com/2011/04/08 /wc11-star-saoirse-ronan-on-hannas-grim-grimms-fairy-tale/.

Roth, Veronica. 2011. *Divergent*. New York: Katherine Tegen Books.

———. 2012. *Insurgent*. New York: Katherine Tegen Books.

———. 2013. *Allegiant*. New York: Katherine Tegen Books.

Rubenfeld, Jed. 2014. "Mishandling Rape." *New York Times*, November 15; see www.nytimes.com/2014/11/16/opinion/sunday/mishandling-rape.html

Sampson, Rana. 2002. "Acquaintance Rape of College Students." In the Problem-Oriented Guides for Police Series, No. 17. U.S. Department of Justice, Office of Community Oriented Policing Services.

Samuels, Mina. 2011. *Run Like a Girl: How Strong Women Make Happy Lives*. Berkeley, CA: Seal Press.

Sanday, Peggy. 1996. *A Woman Scorned*. New York: Doubleday.

——. 2007. *Fraternity Gang Rape: Sex, Brotherhood, and Privilege on Campus*. New York: New York University Press.

Sauers, Jenna. 2012. "Violence Against Women Disguised as 'Fashion.' " *Jezebel*, June 11; see http://jezebel.com/5916650/fashions-ongoing-violence-against -women/.

Schulhofer, Stephen J. 2000. *Unwanted Sex: The Culture of Intimidation and the Failure of Law*. New ed. Cambridge: Harvard University Press.

Schwarz, Alan. 2015. "Sorority Anti-Rape Idea: Drinking on Own Turf." *New York Times*, January 19; see www.nytimes.com/2015/01/20/us/sorority-anti -rape-idea-drinking-on-own-turf.html.

Scully, D. and J. Marolla. 1984. "Convicted Rapists' Vocabulary of Motive: Excuses and Justifications." *Social Problems* 31: 530–44.

Scott, A. O. 2011. " 'The Girl with the Dragon Tattoo'—Review." *New York Times*, December 19; see www.nytimes.com/2011/12/20/movies/the-girl -with-dragon-tattoo-movie-review.html.

Scott, A. O. and Manohla Dargis. 2011. "Women as Violent Characters in Movies." *New York Times*, April 27; see www.nytimes.com/2011/05/01/movies /women-as-violent-characters-in-movies.html.

——. 2014. "Representation of Female Characters in Movies Is Improving." *New York Times*, September 3; see www.nytimes.com/2014/09/07/movies /fall-arts-preview-representation-of-female-characters-in-movies-is-improving .html.

Seltzer, Sarah and Lauren Kelly. 2012. "Eight Staggering GOP Comments on Rape and Women." *Salon*, August 22; see www.salon.com/2012/08/22/eight _staggering_gop_comments_on_rape_and_women/.

She-Wolf of London. 1946. Directed by Jean Yarbrough. Universal City, CA: Universal Studios, 2007, DVD.

Shim, Eileen. 2014. "Teens Allegedly Used Snapchat to Broadcast a 16-Year-Old's Rape." *Mic*, September 25; see http://mic.com/articles/99752/a-mother -claims-her-daughter-s-rape-was-posted-to-snapchat.

Shrek. 2001. Directed by Andrew Adamson and Vicky Jenson. Universal City, CA: DreamWorks Animated, 2011. DVD.

Shulevitz, Judith. 2015. "In College and Hiding from Scary Ideas." *New York Times*, March 21; see www.nytimes.com/2015/03/22/opinion/sunday/judith -shulevitz-hiding-from-scary-ideas.html.

Sivakumaran, Sandesh. 2005. "Male/Male Rape and the 'Taint' of Homosexuality." *Human Rights Quarterly* 27 (4): 1274–1306.

Sleeping Beauty. 1959. Directed by Clyde Geronimi, Les Clark, Eric Larson, and Wolfgang Reitherman. Burbank, CA: Walt Disney Studios Home Entertainment, 2014. DVD.

Smith, S. E. 2014. "Why Did 'Divergent's' Producers Deviate from the Text to Add a Rape Scene?" *xoJane*, March 26; see www.xojane.com/entertainment /divergent-rape-scene.

Snow, Nancy E. 1994. "Self-Blame and Blame of Rape Victims." *Public Affairs Quarterly* 8 (4): 377–93.

Snow White and the Huntsman. 2012. Directed by Rupert Sanders. Universal City, CA: Universal Studios, 2012. DVD.

Snow White and the Seven Dwarfs. 1937. Directed by David Hand, William Cottrell, Wilfred Jackson, Larry Morey, Perce Pearce, and Ben Sharpsteen. Burbank, CA: Walt Disney Video, 2001. DVD.

Southall, Ashley. 2015. "Penn State, Harassment and Hazing, Suspends Recognition of a Fraternity." *New York Times*, May 28, A13.

Species. 1995. Directed by Roger Donaldson. Beverly Hills, CA: MGM, 2006. DVD.

Splice. 2009. Directed by Vincenzo Natali. Burbank, CA: Warner Home Video, 2010. DVD.

Stapleton, AnneClaire, and Josh Levs. 2015. "Alleged Gang Rape on Crowded Beach Is 'Not the First,' Sheriff Says." CNN, April 6; see www.cnn .com/2015/04/14/us/florida-panama-city-gang-rape-case/index.html.

Stein, Joel. 2014. "Will Frat Guys Always Run the World." *Playboy*, September 24; see www.playboy.com/articles/will-frat-guys-rule-the-world.

Stimpson, Catharine R. 2006. "The Atalanta Syndrome: Women, Sports, and Cultural Values." *S&F Online* 4 (3); see http://sfonline.barnard.edu/sport /stimpson_05.htm.

Stotzer, Rebecca L. 2009. "Violence Against Transgender People: A Review of United States Data." *Aggression and Violent Behavior* 14 (3): 170–79.

Stover, Cassandra. 2013. "Damsels and Heroines: The Conundrum of the Post-Feminist Disney Princess." *LUX: A Journal of Transdisciplinary Writing from Claremont University* 2 (1): 1–10.

Sucker Punch. 2011. Directed by Zack Snyder. Burbank, CA: Warner Brothers Studios, 2011. DVD.

Sussens-Messerer, Victoria. 2012. "Five Hundred New Fairy Tales Discovered in Germany." *The Guardian* (England), March 5; see www.theguardian.com /books/2012/mar/05/five-hundred-fairytales-discovered-germany.

Taylor, Jonathan. 2014. "Lips That Lie: 10 Reasons False Rape Claims Are Higher than Two Percent." *A Voice for Male Students.* July 8; see www .avoiceformalestudents.com/avfms-mega-post-10-reasons-false-rape -accusations-are-common/lips-that-lie-a-voice-for-male-students-10 -reasons-false-rape-claims-are-higher-than-two-percent/.

Taylor, Chloë. 2009. "Foucault, Feminism, and Sex Crimes." *Hypatia* 24 (4): 1–25.

———. 2013. "Infamous Men, Dangerous Individuals, and Violence Against Women: Feminist Rereadings of Michel Foucault." In Christopher Falzon, Timothy O'Leary, and Jana Sawicki, eds., *A Companion to Foucault*, 419–35. Malden, MA: Blackwell.

Thomas, Peyton. 2014. "The 'Divergent' Rape Scene: Here's Why It Matters." *Medium*, March 21; see https://medium.com/@silkspectres/the-divergent -rape-scene-heres-why-it-matters-1d20ea8b9064.

Tieger, T. 1981. "Self-Reported Likelihood of Raping and the Social Perception of Rape." *Journal of Research in Personality* 15: 147–58.

Timberg, Craig. 2013. "How Violent Porn Sites Manage to Hide Information That Should Be Public." *Washington Post*, December 6; see www .washingtonpost.com/business/technology/how-violent-porn-sites-manage-to-hide-information-that-should-be-public/2013/12/06/e0861378–3773– 11e3-ae46-e4248e75c8ea_story.html.

Travers, Peter. "Fifty Shades of Grey." 2015. *Rolling Stone*. February 11; see www.rollingstone.com/movies/reviews/fifty-shades-of-grey-20150211.

Tsaros, Angelika. 2013. "Consensual Non-Consent: Comparing E. L. James's *Fifty Shades of Grey* and Pauline Reage's *Story of O*." *Sexulities* 16 (8): 864–79.

Twilight. 2008. Directed by Catherine Hardwicke. Universal City, CA: Summit Entertainment, 2009. DVD.

The Twilight Saga: New Moon. 2009. Directed by Chris Weitz. Universal City, CA: Summit Entertainment, 2010. DVD.

The Twilight Saga: Eclipse. 2010. Directed by David Slade. Universal City, CA: Summit Entertainment, 2010. DVD.

The Twilight Saga: Breaking Dawn—Part 1. 2011. Directed by Bill Condon. Universal City, CA: Summit Entertainment, 2012. DVD.

The Twilight Saga: Breaking Dawn—Part 2. 2012. Directed by Bill Condon. Universal City, CA: Summit Entertainment, 2013. DVD.

Ullman, Sarah E. and Liana Peter-Hagene. 2014. "Social Reactions to Sexual Assault Disclosure, Coping, Perceived Control, and PTSD Symptoms in Sexual Assault Victims." *Journal of Community Psychology* 42 (4): 495–508.

Unfriended. Directed by Levan Gabriadze. Universal City, CA: Universal Pictures. 2015. DVD.

United States Department of Education. 2011. "Dear Colleague Letter: Sexual Violence, Background, Summary, and Fast Facts." April 4, 2011; see www2 .ed.gov/about/offices/list/ocr/docs/dcl-factsheet-201104.html (last accessed June 15, 2015).

Valby, Karen. 2013. "The Hunger Games Catching Fire." *Entertainment Weekly Magazine*, January 18.

Warner, Marina. 1994. "Absent Mothers." In *From the Beast to the Blonde*. New York: Farrar, Strauss, Giroux.

Warshaw, Robin. 1994. *I Never Called It Rape: The Ms. Report on Recognizing, Fighting, and Surviving Date and Acquaintance Rape*. Rpt. ed. New York: Harper Perennial.

The Wasp Woman. 1959. Directed by Roger Corman and Jack Hill. Universal City, CA: Gaiam Vivendi Entertainment, 2005. DVD.

Wertheimer, Alan. 2003. *Consent to Sexual Relations*. New York: Cambridge University Press.

West, R. 1996. "A Comment on Sex, Consent, and Rape." *Legal Theory* 2: 233–51.

Westen, Peter. 2004. *The Logic of Consent: The Diversity and Deceptiveness of Consent As a Defense to Criminal Conduct*. Burlington, VT: Ashgate.

Whale Rider. 2003. Directed by Niki Caro. Santa Monica, CA: Lionsgate, 2011. DVD.

Whisnant, Rebecca. 2007. "A Woman's Body Is Like a Foreign Country: Thinking About National and Bodily Sovereignty." In Peggy DesAutels and Rebecca Whisnant, eds., *Global Feminist Ethics*, 155–76. Lanham, MD: Rowman and Littlefield.

——. 2013. "Feminist Perspectives on Rape." In Edward N. Zalta, ed., *The Stanford Encyclopedia of Philosophy*; see http://plato.stanford.edu/archives /fall2013/entries/feminism-rape/.

White, Sandy and Niwako Yamawaki. 2009. "The Moderating Influence of Homophobia and Gender–Role Traditionality on Perceptions of Male Rape Victims 1." *Journal of Applied Social Psychology* 39 (5): 1116–36.

Whitlock, Craig. 2012. "Air Force Investigates Growing Sex-Abuse Scandal." *Washington Post*, June 28; see www.washingtonpost.com/world/national-security/air-force-investigates-growing-sex-abuse-scandal/2012/06/28/gJQA utm39V_story.html?tid=pm_world_pop.

——. 2013. "Pentagon Grapples with Sex Crimes by Military Recruiters." *Washington Post*, May 12; see www.washingtonpost.com/world/national-security /pentagon-grapples-with-sex-crimes-by-military-recruiters/2013/05/12 /d082ec1c-b97e-11e2-bd07-b6e0e6152528_story.html?Post+generic =%3Ftid%3Dsm_twitter_washingtonpost.

Williams, Mary Elizabeth. 2013. "College Students Cheer Sex Abuse." September 5; see www.salon.com/2013/09/05/college_students_cheer_sex_abuse/.

Winter's Bone. 2010. Directed by Debra Granik. Santa Monica, CA: Lionsgate, 2010. DVD.

The Wizard of Oz. 1939. Directed by Victor Fleming. Warner Brothers, 2013. DVD.

Wolfe, Tom. 2000. *Hooking Up*. New York: Farrar, Straus, and Giroux.

Wolitzky-Taylor, Kate B., Heidi S. Resnick, Ananda B. Amstadter, Jenna L. Mccauley, Kenneth J. Ruggiero, and Dean G. Kilpatrick. 2011. "Reporting Rape in a National Sample of College Women." *Journal of American College Health* 59 (7): 582–87.

Yaeger, Deborah, Naomi Himmelfarb, Alison Cammack, and Jim Mintz. 2006. "DSM-IV Diagnosed Posttraumatic Stress Disorder in Women Veterans with and without Military Sexual Trauma." *Journal of General Internal Medicine* 21 (Supplement 3): S65-S69.

Yzer, M. C., F. W. Siero, and B. P. Buunk. 1999. "Can Public Campaigns Effectively Change Psychological Determinants of Safer Sex? An Evaluation of Three Dutch Campaigns." *Health Education Research* 15 (3): 339–52.

Zorza, Joan. 2001. "Drug-Facilitated Rape." In Allen J. Ottens and Kathy Hotelling, eds., *Sexual Violence on Campus: Policies, Programs, and Perspectives*, 53–75. New York: Springer.

INDEX